DIESTERWEGS
NEUSPRACHLICHE
BIBLIOTHEK

W0314516

Sue Townsend

The Secret Diary of Adrian Mole Aged 13¾

Edited and annotated
by
Friedrich Klein

VERLAG MORITZ DIESTERWEG
Frankfurt am Main

Abbreviations

cf.	compare	*BE*	British English
e.g.	for example	*contempt.*	contemptuous
esp.	especially	*inf.*	informal
s.o.	someone	*fml.*	formal
s.th.	something	*sl.*	slang
o.s.	oneself	*fig.*	figurative
G.	German	*arch.*	archaic
AE	American English		

Copyright © 1982 Sue Townsend

ISBN 3-425-04004-9

© 1990 Verlag Moritz Diesterweg GmbH & Co., Frankfurt am Main.
Alle Rechte vorbehalten. Das Werk und seine Teile sind urheberrechtlich geschützt.
Jede Verwertung in anderen als den gesetzlich zugelassenen Fällen
bedarf deshalb der vorherigen schriftlichen Einwilligung des Verlags.

Satz: Karlheinz Stahringer, Ebsdorfergrund
Druck: graphoprint, Koblenz
Printed in Germany

For Colin
and also for Sean,
Dan, Vicki and Elizabeth
with love and thanks

"Paul walked with something screwed up tight* inside him ... yet he chatted* away with his mother. He would never have confessed* to her how he suffered over these things and she only partly* guessed."

D. H. Lawrence* *Sons and Lovers**

to be screwed up tight *here: G.* angespannt sein **to chat** *inf.* to talk in a friendly way **to confess** to make s.th. known, to tell **partly** in part **D. H. Lawrence** (1885–1930) a British writer whose autobiographical novel *Sons and Lovers* (1913) shows the personal conflicts and problems of a young man

Thursday January 1st

BANK HOLIDAY* IN ENGLAND, IRELAND, SCOTLAND AND WALES

These are my New Year's resolutions*:

1. I will help the blind across the road.
2. I will hang my trousers up.
3. I will put the sleeves* back on my records.
4. I will not start smoking.
5. I will stop squeezing my spots*.
6. I will be kind to the dog.
7. I will help the poor and ignorant.
8. After hearing the disgusting noises from downstairs last night, I have also vowed* never to drink alcohol.

My father got the dog drunk on cherry brandy at the party last night. If the RSPCA* hear about it he could get done*. Eight days have gone by since Christmas Day but my mother still hasn't worn the green lurex* apron I bought her for Christmas! She will get bathcubes* next year.

Just my luck, I've got a spot on my chin for the first day of the New Year!

Friday January 2nd

BANK HOLIDAY IN SCOTLAND. FULL MOON

I felt rotten today. It's my mother's fault for singing "My Way" at two o'clock in the morning at the top of the stairs. Just my luck to have a mother like her. There is a chance my parents could be alcoholics. Next year I could be in a children's home.

The dog got its own back* on my father. It jumped up and knocked down his model ship, then ran into the garden with the rigging* tangled* in its feet. My father kept saying, "Three months' work down the drain*", over and over again.

The spot on my chin is getting bigger. It's my mother's fault for not knowing about vitamins.

bank holiday public holiday in the UK when banks, shops and factories are closed **resolution** decision **sleeve** *here:* cover **spot** *G.* Pickel **to vow** [vaʊ] *G.* geloben **RSPCA** Royal Society for the Prevention of Cruelty to Animals (*G.* Tierschutzverein) **to get done** *inf.* to get arrested **lurex** ['lʊərɜks] (trademark) made of aluminium and plastic **cube** [kju:b] *G.* Würfel **to get one's own back** *inf.* to take revenge successfully **rigging** *G.* Takelage **tangled** *G.* verheddert **down the drain** *inf. fig. G.* zunichte gemacht, vergeudet (drain *G.* Abflussrohr, Gully)

Saturday January 3rd

I shall go mad through lack of* sleep! My father has banned the dog from the house so it barked outside my window all night. Just my luck! My father shouted a swear-word* at it. If he's not careful he will get done by the police for obscene language.

I think the spot is a boil*. Just my luck to have it where everybody can see it. I pointed out to my mother that I hadn't had any vitamin C today. She said, "Go and buy an orange, then". This is typical.

She still hasn't worn the lurex apron.

I will be glad to get back to school.

Sunday January 4th
SECOND AFTER CHRISTMAS

My father has got the flu. I'm not surprised with the diet* we get. My mother went out in the rain to get him a vitamin C drink, but as I told her, "It's too late now". It's a miracle* we don't get scurvy*. My mother says she can't see anything on my chin, but this is guilt* because of the diet.

The dog has run off because my mother didn't close the gate. I have broken the arm on the stereo. Nobody knows yet, and with a bit of luck my father will be ill for a long time. He is the only one who uses it apart from me. No sign of the apron.

Monday January 5th

The dog hasn't come back yet. It is peaceful without it. My mother rang the police and gave a description of the dog. She made it sound worse than it actually is: straggly* hair over its eyes and all that. I really think the police have got better things to do than look for dogs, such as catching murderers. I told my mother this but she still rang them. Serve her right* if she was murdered because of the dog.

My father is still lazing* about in bed. He is supposed to be ill, but I noticed he is still smoking!

Nigel came round today. He has got a tan* from his Christmas holiday.

lack of being without **swear-word** *G.* Fluch **boil** *G.* Furunkel **diet** ['daɪət] *G.* Nahrung, Kost **miracle** *G.* Wunder **scurvy** ['skɜːvɪ] *G.* Skorbut (schwerer Vitaminmangel) **guilt** *here: G.* Schuldgefühl **straggly** growing in an untidy manner **serve her right** *inf. short for* it would serve her right (*G.* es geschähe ihr recht) **to laze** to be lazy **tan** *G.* Bräune

I think Nigel will be ill soon from the shock of the cold in England. I think Nigel's parents were wrong to take him abroad.

He hasn't got a single spot yet.

Tuesday January 6th

EPIPHANY*. NEW MOON

The dog is in trouble!

It knocked a meter-reader* off his bike and messed* all the cards up. So now we will all end up in court I expect. A policeman said we must keep the dog under control and asked how long it had been lame. My mother said it wasn't lame, and examined it. There was a tiny model pirate trapped* in its left front paw*.

The dog was pleased when my mother took the pirate out and it jumped up the policeman's tunic* with its muddy paws. My mother fetched a cloth from the kitchen but it had strawberry jam on it where I had wiped the kife, so the tunic was worse than ever. The policeman went then. I'm sure he swore. I could report him for that.

I will look up "Epiphany" in my new dictionary.

Wednesday January 7th

Nigel came round on his new bike this morning. It has got a water bottle, a milometer*, a speedometer, a yellow saddle, and very thin racing wheels. It's wasted on Nigel. He only goes to the shops and back on it. If I had it, I would go all over the country and have an experience.

My spot or boil has reached its peak*. Surely it can't get any bigger!

I found a word in my dictionary that describes my father. It is *malingerer**. He is still in bed guzzling* vitamin C.

The dog is locked in the coal shed.

Epiphany is something to do with the three wise men. Big deal*!

epiphany [ɪ'pɪfənɪ] (= manifestation) *here:* the day when Jesus Christ as a baby was visited by the three magi, three wise men from the East **meter-reader** *G.* Kontrolleur, der Gas- und Wasseruhren abliest **to mess up** *inf.* to make s.th. very untidy and dirty **to trap** to catch **paw** [pɔː] foot of a dog, cat, etc. **tunic** uniform jacket **milometer** [maɪ'lɒmɪtə] *G.* Tacho **peak** highest point **malingerer** [mə'lɪŋgərə] s.o. who pretends to be ill in order to avoid work **to guzzle** *inf.* to drink quickly and thirstily **big deal** *here: inf. G.* "Ist ja umwerfend!"

Thursday January 8th

Now my mother has got the flu. This means that I have to look after them both. Just my luck!

I have been up and down the stairs all day. I cooked a big dinner for them tonight: two poached eggs* with beans, and tinned* semolina* pudding. (It's a good job I wore the green lurex apron because the poached eggs escaped out of the pan and got all over me.) I nearly said something when I saw they hadn't eaten *any* of it. They can't be that ill. I gave it to the dog in the coal shed. My grandmother is coming tomorrow morning, so I had to clean the burnt saucepans, then take the dog for a walk. It was half-past eleven before I got to bed. No wonder I am short for my age.

I have decided against medicine for a career.

Friday January 9th

It was cough, cough, cough last night. If it wasn't one it was the other. You'd think they'd show some consideration* after the hard day I'd had.

My grandma came and was disgusted with* the state of the house. I showed her my room which is always neat and tidy and she gave me fifty pence. I showed her all the empty drink bottles in the dustbin and she was disgusted*.

My grandma let the dog out of the coal shed. She said my mother was cruel to lock it up. The dog was sick* on the kitchen floor. My grandma locked it up again.

She squeezed the spot on my chin. It has made it worse. I told grandma about the green apron and grandma said that she bought my mother a one hundred per cent acrylic cardigan* every Christmas and my mother had *never ever* worn one of them!

Saturday January 10th

a.m. Now the dog is ill! It keeps being sick so the vet* has got to come. My father told me not to tell the vet that the dog had been locked in the coal shed for two days.

poached egg an egg that is boiled gently without its shell **to tin** *BE* to put in a tin
semolina [ˌseməˈliːnə] *G.* Grieß **consideration** [kənˌsɪdəˈreɪʃn] *G.* Rücksichtnahme
to be disgusted *G.* angeekelt sein **to be sick** *BE* to throw up (*G.* sich übergeben)
cardigan woollen jacket **vet** *short for:* veterinary surgeon (*G.* Tierarzt)

ster over the spot to stop germs* getting in it from the

en the dog away. He says he thinks it has got an ob- need an emergency operation.

s had a row* with my mother and gone home. My Christmas cardigans all cut up in the duster* bag. It people are starving*.

xt door has been in to see my mother and father who brought a "get well" card and some flowers for my sat up in bed in a nightie* that showed a lot of her Mr Lucas in a yukky* voice. My father pretended to

ecords round. He is into* punk, but I don't see the the words. Anyway I think I'm turning into an in- ll the worry.

how the dog is. It has had its operation. The vet stic bag with lots of yukky things in it. There was a lump* of coal, the fir tree from the Christmas cake, and the model pirates from my father's ship. One of the pirates was waving a cutlass* which must have been very painful for the dog. The dog looks a lot better. It can come home in two days, worse luck.

My father was having a row with my grandma on the phone about the empty bottles in the dustbin when I got home.

Mr Lucas was upstairs talking to my mother. When Mr Lucas went, my father went upstairs and had an argument with* my mother and made her cry. My father is in a bad mood. This means he is feeling better. I made my mother a cup of tea without her asking. This made her cry as well. You can't please some people!

The spot is still there.

germ *G.* Bakterie **obstruction** [əbˈstrʌkʃn] *here: G.* Verstopfung **row** [raʊ] *here:* quarrel, fight **duster** *G.* Staubtuch **to starve** [stɑːv] to be without food **nightie** [ˈnaɪtɪ] *inf.* nightdress **chest** *G.* Brust **yukky** *inf. contempt.* (this word shows that one does not like s.th.) **to be into** *inf.* to be very interested in **lump** a hard piece **cutlass** *G.* Entermesser **to have an argument with** to quarrel with

Sunday January 11th

FIRST* AFTER EPIPHANY

Now I *know* I am an intellectual. I saw Malcom Muggeridge* on the television last night, and I understood nearly every word. It all adds up. A bad home, poor diet, not liking punk. I think I will join the library and see what happens.

It is a pity there aren't any more intellectuals living round here. Mr Lucas wears corduroy* trousers, but he's an insurance* man. Just my luck.

The first what after Epiphany?

Monday January 12th

The dog is back. It keeps licking* its stitches*, so when I am eating I sit with my back to it.

My mother got up this morning to make the dog a bed to sleep in until it's better. It is made out of a cardboard box that used to contain packets of soap powder. My father said this would make the dog sneeze and burst its stitches, and the vet would charge even more to stitch it back up again. They had a row about the box, then my father went on about* Mr Lucas. Though what Mr Lucas has to do with the dog's bed is a mystery to me.

Tuesday January 13th

My father has gone back to work. Thank God! I don't know how my mother sticks* him.

Mr Lucas came in this morning to see if my mother needed any help in the house. He is very kind. Mrs Lucas was next door cleaning the outside windows. The ladder didn't look very safe. I have written to Malcolm Muggeridge, c/o* the BBC, asking him what to do about being an intellectual. I hope he writes back soon because I'm getting fed up being one on my own. I have written a poem, and it only took me two minutes. Even the famous poets take longer than that. It is called "The Tap*", but it isn't really about a tap, it's very deep, and about life and stuff like that.

first *here:* first Sunday **epiphany** [ɪ'pɪfənɪ] *cf. p. 7* **Malcolm Muggeridge** British TV personality and journalist **corduroy** *G.* Kord- **insurance** [ɪn'ʃʊərəns] *G.* Versicherung **to lick** *G.* lecken **stitch** *here: G.* Faden **to go on about s. th.** *inf.* to talk about s. th. all the time **to stick s. o.** *inf.* to stand s. o. (*G.* jem. ertragen) **c/o** *short for:* care of (*G.* bei; zu Händen von) **tap** *G.* Wasserhahn

The Tap, by Adrian Mole
The tap drips and keeps me awake,
In the morning there will be a lake.
For the want of* a washer* the carpet will spoil,
Then for another my father will toil*.
My father could snuff it* while he is at work.
Dad, fit a washer don't be a burk*!

I showed it to my mother, but she laughed. She isn't very bright. She still hasn't washed my PE* shorts, and it is school tomorrow. She is not like the mothers on television.

Wednesday January 14th

Joined the library. Got *Care of the Skin, Origin of Species**, and a book by a woman my mother is always going on about. It is called *Pride and Prejudice**, by a woman called Jane Austen*. I could tell the librarian was impressed. Perhaps she is an intellectual like me. She didn't look at my spot, so perhaps it is getting smaller. About time!

Mr Lucas was in the kitchen drinking coffee with my mother. The room was full of smoke. They were laughing, but when I went in, they stopped.

Mrs Lucas was next door cleaning the drains*. She looked as if she was in a bad mood. I think Mr and Mrs Lucas have got an unhappy marriage. Poor Mr Lucas!

None of the teachers at school have noticed that I am an intellectual. They will be sorry when I am famous. There is a new girl in our class. She sits next to me in Geography. She is all right. Her name is Pandora*, but she likes being called "Box*". Don't ask me why. I might fall in love with her. It's time I fell in love, after all I am 13 3/4 years old.

for the want of s.th. because of the absence of s.th. **washer** *here: G.* Dichtungsring **to toil** *fml.* to work very hard **to snuff it** *BE inf. here:* to die **burk** [bɜːk] *BE sl.* fool, idiot **bright** *here:* clever **PE** *short for:* Physical Education (*G.* Sportunterricht) **(On the) Origin of Species** ['spiːʃiːz] a book by Charles Darwin (1809–1882) about the way life has developed on our planet (evolution theory) **Pride and Prejudice** ['predʒʊdɪs] (*G.* Stolz und Vorurteil) a famous novel by **Jane Austen** ['ɒstɪn] (1775–1817) **drain** *G.* Abflussrohr, Gully **Pandora** in Greek legend, the name of the first woman, whom the gods gave a **box** as a wedding present; when she opened the box, out came all the problems and diseases which are now in the world

Thursday January 15th

Pandora has got hair the colour of treacle*, and it's long like girls' hair should be. She has quite a good figure. I saw her playing netball* and her chest was wobbling*. I felt a bit funny. I think this is it!

The dog has had its stitches out. It bit the vet, but I expect he's used to* it. (The vet I mean; I know the dog is.)

My father found out about the arm on the stereo. I told a lie. I said the dog jumped up and broke it. My father said he will wait until the dog is completely cured* of its operation then kick it. I hope this is a joke.

Mr Lucas was in the kitchen again when I got home from school. My mother is better now, so why he keeps coming round is a mystery to me. Mrs Lucas was planting trees in the dark. I read a bit of *Pride and Prejudice*, but it was very old-fashioned*. I think Jane Austen should write something a bit more modern.

The dog has got the same colour eyes as Pandora. I only noticed because my mother cut the dog's hair. It looks worse than ever. Mr Lucas and my mother were laughing at the dog's new haircut which is not very nice, because dogs can't answer back, just like the Royal Family.

I am going to bed early to think about Pandora and do my back-stretching exercises. I haven't grown for two weeks. If this carries on I will be a midget*.

I will go to the doctor's on Saturday if the spot is still there. I can't live like this with everybody staring.

Friday January 16th

Mr Lucas came round and offered to take my mother shopping in the car. They dropped me off at school. I was glad to get out of the car what with all the laughing and cigarette smoke. We saw Mrs Lucas on the way. She was carrying big bags of shopping. My mother waved, but Mrs Lucas couldn't wave back.

It was Geography today so I sat next to Pandora for a whole hour. She looks better every day. I told her about her eyes being the same as the dog's. She asked what kind of dog it was. I told her it was a mongrel*.

I lent Pandora my blue felt-tip pen to colour round the British Isles.

treacle ['tri:kl] *G.* Sirup, Melasse **netball** a game like basketball, mainly played by women **to wobble** to move from side to side **to be used to s. th.** *G.* an etwas gewöhnt sein **to cure** ['kjʊə] to make healthy again **old-fashioned** *G.* altmodisch **midget** ['mɪdʒɪt] a very small person **mongrel** ['mʌŋgrəl] *G.* Promenadenmischung

I think she appreciates* these small attentions.

I started *Origin of Species* today, but it's not as good as the television series. *Care of the Skin* is dead* good. I have left it open on the pages about vitamins. I hope my mother takes the hint*. I have left it on the kitchen table near the ashtray, so she is bound to see it.

I have made an appointment about the spot. It has turned purple.

Saturday January 17th

I was woken up early this morning. Mrs Lucas is concreting* the front of their house and the concrete lorry had to keep its engine running while she shovelled* the concrete round before it set*. Mr Lucas made her a cup of tea. He really is kind.

Nigel came round to see if I wanted to go to the pictures* but I told him I couldn't, because I was going to the doctor's about the spot. He said he couldn't see a spot, but he was just being polite because the spot is massive today.

Dr Taylor must be one of those overworked GPs* you are always reading about. He didn't examine the spot, he just said I mustn't worry and was everything all right at home. I told him about my bad home life and my poor diet, but he said I was well nourished* and to go home and count my blessings*. So much for the National Health Service.

I will get a paper-round and go private.

Sunday January 18th

SECOND AFTER EPIPHANY, OXFORD HILARY TERM* STARTS

Mrs Lucas and my mother have had a row over the dog. Somehow it escaped from the house and trampled on Mrs Lucas's wet concrete. My father offered to have the dog put down*, but my mother started to cry so he said he wouldn't. All the neighbours were out in the street washing their cars and listening. Sometimes I really hate that dog!

to appreciate *G.* (wert)schätzen **dead** *here inf. adverb!* very **to take a hint** *G.* einen Wink verstehen **to concrete** *G.* betonieren **to shovel** ['ʃʌvl] *G.* schaufeln, schippen **to set** *here:* to become heavy **to go to the pictures** *BE* to go to the cinema **GP** *short for:* General Practitioner (a doctor who is trained in general medicine) **to nourish** ['nʌrɪʃ] to feed good food **to count one's blessings** to think only about one's good things **Hilary term** spring term at Oxford University **to put an animal down** to kill an old or sick animal

I remembered my resolution about helping the poor and ignorant today, so I took some of my old *Beano** annuals* to a quite poor family who have moved into the next street. I know they are poor because they have only got a black and white telly*. A boy answered the door. I explained why I had come. He looked at the annuals and said, "I've read 'em", and slammed* the door in my face. So much for helping the poor!

Monday January 19th

I have joined a group at school called the Good Samaritans. We go out into the community* helping and stuff like that. We miss Maths on Monday afternoons.

Today we had a talk on the sort of things we will be doing. I have been put in the old age pensioners'* group. Nigel has got a dead yukky job looking after kids in a playgroup. He is as sick as a parrot.

I can't wait for next Monday. I will get a cassette so I can tape all the old fogies'* stories about the war and stuff*. I hope I get one with a good memory.

The dog is back at the vet's. It has got concrete stuck on its paws. No wonder it was making such a row on the stairs last night. Pandora smiled at me in school dinner today, but I was choking* on a piece of gristle* so I couldn't smile back. Just my luck!

Tuesday January 20th

FULL MOON

My mother is looking for a job!

Now I could end up a delinquent* roaming* the streets and all that. And what will I do during the holidays? I expect I will have to sit in a launderette* all day to keep warm. I will be a latchkey kid*, whatever that is. And who will look after the dog? And what will I have to eat all day? I will be forced to eat crisps and sweets until my skin is ruined and my teeth fall out. I think my mother is being very selfish. She won't be

Beano *BE* ['bi:nəʊ] name of a popular weekly comic for children **annual** ['ænjʊəl] *G.* Jahresband, Jahrgang **telly** *inf.* television **to slam** *G.* zuschlagen, zuknallen **community** [kə'mju:nətɪ] *G.* Gemeinschaft, Gemeinde **old age pensioner** (*short:* OAP) an old person who does not work any more and gets a pension from the state **fogy/fogey** ['fəʊgɪ] *inf.* an old-fashioned person **and stuff** *inf.* and things like that (stuff *G.* Zeug) **to choke** *G.* ersticken, würgen **gristle** *G.* Knorpel **delinquent** [dɪ'lɪŋkwənt] (young) criminal **to roam** [rəʊm] to wander about **launderette** a shop where people can use washing machines **latchkey kid** *G.* Schlüsselkind

any good in a job anyway. She isn't bright and she drinks too much at Christmas.

I rang my grandma up and told her, and she says I could stay at her house in the holidays, and go to the Evergreens' meetings* in the afternoons and stuff like that. I wish I hadn't rung now. The Samaritans met today during break. The old people were shared out*. I got an old man called Bert Baxter. He is eighty-nine so I don't suppose I'll have him for long. I'm going round to see him tomorrow. I hope he hasn't got a dog. I'm fed up with dogs. They are either at the vet's or standing in front of the televison.

Wednesday   January 21st

Mr and Mrs Lucas are getting a divorce*! They are the first down our road. My mother went next door to comfort* Mr Lucas. He must have been very upset* because she was still there when my father came home from work. Mrs Lucas has gone somewhere in a taxi. I think she has left for ever because she has taken her socket* set with her. Poor Mr Lucas, now he will have to do his own washing and stuff.

My father cooked the tea tonight. We had boil-in-the-bag curry and rice, it was the only thing left in the freezer apart from a bag of green stuff which has lost its label*. My father made a joke about sending it to the public health inspector. My mother didn't laugh. Perhaps she was thinking about poor Mr Lucas left on his own.

I went to see old Mr Baxter after tea. My father dropped me off on his way to play badminton. Mr Baxter's house is hard to see from the road. It has got a massive overgrown privet hedge* all round it. When I knocked on the door a dog started barking and growling and jumping up at the letterbox. I heard the sound of bottles being knocked over and a man swearing before I ran off. I hope I got the wrong number.

I saw Nigel on the way home. He told me Pandora's father is a milkman! I have gone off* her a bit.

Nobody was in when I got home so I fed the dog, looked at my spots and went to bed.

Evergreens a club for old people **to share out** to divide **divorce** *G.* Ehescheidung **to comfort s.o.** to cheer s.o. up **upset** very worried and unhappy **socket (spanner)** *here: G.* Schraubenschlüssel **label** *G.* Etikett **privet** ['prɪvɪt] **hedge** *G.* Ligusterhecke **to go off s.o.** *inf.* to stop liking s.o.

Thursday January 22nd

It is a dirty lie about Pandora's father being a milkman! He is an accountant* at the dairy*. Pandora says she will duff* Nigel up if he goes round committing libel*. I am in love with her again.

Nigel has asked me to go to a disco at the youth club tomorrow night; it is being held to raise funds* for a new packet of ping-pong balls. I don't know if I will go because Nigel is a punk at weekends. His mother lets him be one providing* he wears a string vest* under his bondage T-shirt*.

My mother has got an interview for a job. She is practising her typing and not doing any cooking. So what will it be like if she *gets* the job? My father should put his foot down* before we are a broken home.

Friday January 23rd

That is the last time I go to a disco. Everybody there was a punk except me and Rick Lemon, the youth leader. Nigel was showing off* all night. He ended up putting a safety pin through his ear. My father had to take him to the hospital in our car. Nigel's parents haven't got a car because his father's got a steel plate in his head and his mother is only four feet eleven inches tall. It's not surprising Nigel has turned out bad really, with a maniac* and a midget* for parents.

I still haven't heard from Malcolm Muggeridge. Perhaps he is in a bad mood*. Intellectuals like him and me often have bad moods. Ordinary people don't understand us and say we are sulking*, but we're not.

Pandora has been to see Nigel in hospital. He has got a bit of blood poisoning* from the safety pin. Pandora thinks Nigel is dead* brave. I think he is dead stupid.

I have had a headache all day because of my mother's rotten* typing, but I'm not complaining. I must go to sleep now. I've got to go and see Bert Baxter tomorrow at his house. It was the right number WORSE LUCK!

accountant *G.* Buchhalter(in) **dairy** ['deərɪ] *G.* Molkerei **to duff s.o. up** *BE sl.* to beat s.o. up **to commit libel** *fml.* to tell lies about s.o. **to raise** *here:* to collect, to get **fund** *here:* a sum of money **providing** only if **string vest** *G.* Netzhemd **bondage T-shirt** black shirt worn by punks **to put one's foot down** *inf.* to speak firmly **to show off** *G.* angeben **maniac** ['meɪnɪæk] a dangerously mad person **midget** *cf. p. 12* **to be in a bad mood** *G.* schlecht gelaunt sein **to sulk** *G.* schmollen **poisoning** *G.* Vergiftung **dead** *cf. p. 13* **rotten** *inf.* very bad and unpleasant

Saturday January 24th

Today was the most terrible day of my life. My mother has got a job doing her rotten typing in an insurance office! She starts on Monday! Mr Lucas works at the same place. He is going to give her a lift every day.

And my father is in a bad mood – he thinks his big-end* is going.

But worst of all, Bert Baxter is not a nice old age pensioner! He drinks and smokes and has an Alsatian dog* called Sabre. Sabre was locked in the kitchen while I was cutting the massive hedge, but he didn't stop growling* once.

But even worse than that! Pandora is going out with Nigel!!!!! I think I will never get over this shock.

Sunday January 25th

THIRD AFTER EPIPHANY

10 a.m. I am ill with all the worry, too weak to write much. Nobody has noticed I haven't eaten any breakfast.

2 p.m. Had two junior aspirins at midday and rallied* a bit. Perhaps when I am famous and my diary is discovered people will understand the torment* of being a 13 3/4-year-old undiscovered intellectual.

6 p.m. Pandora! My lost love!

Now I will never stroke* your treacle hair! (Although my blue felt-tip is still at your disposal.)

8 p.m. Pandora! Pandora! Pandora!

10 p.m. Why? Why? Why?

Midnight. Had a crab-paste* sandwich and a satsuma* (for the good of my skin). Feel a bit better. I hope Nigel falls off his bike and is squashed flat* by a lorry. I will never speak to him again. He knew I was in love with Pandora! If I'd had a racing bike for Christmas instead of a lousy* digital stereo alarm clock, none of this would have happened.

big-end *G.* (beim Auto:) Endstück einer Kurbelstange **Alsatian** [æl'seɪʃjən] **dog** a large dog (like a wolf) **to growl** ['graʊl] *G.* knurren **to rally** *here:* to become strong again, to recover **torment** ['--] some very great pain/suffering **to stroke** *G.* streicheln **paste** *G.* Brotaufstrich **satsuma** ['sætsʊmə] *BE* tangerine (*G.* Mandarine) **to squash flat** to press flat, to crush **lousy** ['laʊzɪ] *inf.* bad, unpleasant

Monday January 26th

I had to leave my sick-bed to visit Bert Baxter before school. It took me ages* to get there, what with feeling weak and having to stop for a rest every now and again, but with the help of an old lady who had a long black moustache* I made it to the front door. Bert Baxter was in bed but he threw the key down and I let myself in. Sabre was locked in the bathroom; he was growling and sounded as if he was ripping up towels* or something.

Bert Baxter was lying in a filthy*-looking bed smoking a cigarette, there was a horrible smell in the room, I think it came from Bert Baxter himself. The bed sheets looked as though they were covered in blood, but Bert said that was caused by the beetroot* sandwiches he always eats last thing at night. It was the most disgusting room I have ever seen (and I'm no stranger to squalor*). Bert Baxter gave me ten pence and asked me to get him the *Morning Star** from the newsagent's. So he is a communist as well as everything else! Sabre usually fetches the paper but he is being kept in as a punishment* for chewing* the sink*.

The man in the newsagent's asked me to give Bert Baxter his bill (he owes for his papers, £ 31.97), but when I did Bert Baxter said, "Smarmy* four-eyed git*", and laughed and ripped the bill up. I was late for school so I had to go to the school secretary's office and have my name put in the late book. That's the gratitude* I get for being a Good Samaritan! I didn't miss Maths either! Saw Pandora and Nigel standing close together in the dinner queue but chose to ignore them.

Mr Lucas has taken to his bed because of being deserted* so my mother is taking care of him when she finishes work. She is the only person he will see. So when will she find time to look after me and my father?

My father is sulking. I think he must be jealous* because Mr Lucas doesn't want to see *him*.

Midnight. Goodnight Pandora my treacle-haired love.

XXXXXXXXX*

to take ages *inf. G.* Ewigkeiten dauern **moustache** [mʊˈstɑːʃ] *G.* Schnurrbart **towel** *G.* Handtuch **filthy** very dirty **beetroot** [ˈbiːtruːt] *G.* Rote Bete, Rübe **squalor** [ˈskwɒlə] dirt, untidiness **Morning Star** name of the British communist newspaper **punishment** *G.* Bestrafung **to chew** to keep biting **sink** *G.* Spülbecken, Ausguss **smarmy** *BE inf.* falsely polite **git** *BE sl.* unpleasant person **gratitude** [ˈɡrætɪtjuːd] thankfulness **to desert** [dɪˈzɜːt] to leave s.o. alone who needs help **jealous** [ˈdʒeləs] *G.* eifersüchtig **X** on cards or letters short for: Kiss

Tuesday January 27th

Art was dead good today. I painted a lonely boy standing on a bridge. The boy had just lost his first love to his ex-best friend. The ex-best friend was struggling* in the torrential* river. The boy was watching his ex-best friend drown*. The ex-best friend looked a bit like Nigel. The boy looked a bit like me. Ms Fossington-Gore said my picture "had depth", so did the river. Ha! Ha! Ha!

Wednesday January 28th
LAST QUARTER*

I woke up with a bit of a cold this morning. I asked my mother for a note to excuse me from Games. She said she refused to namby-pamby* me a day longer! How would she like to run about on a muddy field in the freezing drizzle*, dressed only in PE shorts and a singlet*? When I was in the school sports day three-legged race* last year she came to watch me, *and* she had her fur* coat on *and* she put a blanket round her legs, *and* it was only June! Anyway my mother is sorry now, we had rugger* and my PE stuff was so full of mud that it has clogged up the drain hose* on the washing machine.

The vet rang up to demand that we come and fetch the dog back from his surgery*. It has been there nine days. My father says it will have to stay there until he gets paid tomorrow. The vet only takes cash and my father hasn't got any.

Pandora! Why?

Thursday January 29th

The stupid dog is back. I am not taking it for a walk until its hair grows back on its shaved paws. My father looked pale when he came home from the vet's, he kept saying "It's money down the drain", and he said that from now on the dog can only be fed on leftovers from his plate.

This means the dog will soon starve*.

to struggle to fight **torrential** [tə'renʃl] rushing violently **to drown** to die under water because one cannot breathe **last quarter** *here: G.* Halbmond **to namby-pamby** [ˌnæmbɪ'pæmbɪ] *inf.* to treat like a baby **drizzle** very light and fine rain **singlet** *BE* short shirt without sleeves (sleeve *G.* Ärmel) **three-legged** [ˌθriː'legɪd] **race** in this race, you have to run with one of your legs tied to another person's leg **fur** [fɜː] animal skin with soft hair on it **rugger** *coll.* rugby **to clog up the drain hose** [həʊz] *G.* den Abflussschlauch verstopfen **surgery** ['sɜːdʒərɪ] *BE* doctor's room where the patients come to see him **to starve** to be without food, to die of hunger

Friday January 30th

That filthy commie* Bert Baxter has phoned the school to complain that I left the hedge-clippers* out in the rain! He claims that they have gone all rusty. He wants compensation*. I told Mr Scruton, the headmaster, that they were already rusty but I could tell he didn't believe me. He gave me a lecture* on how hard it was for old people to make ends meet*. He has ordered me to go to Bert Baxter's and clean and sharpen the hedge-clippers. I wanted to tell the headmaster all about horrible Bert Baxter but there is something about Mr Scruton that makes my mind go blank. I think it's the way his eyes pop out when he is in a temper*.

On the way to Bert Baxter's I saw my mother and Mr Lucas coming out of a betting shop* together. I waved and shouted but I don't think they could have seen me. I'm glad Mr Lucas is feeling better. Bert Baxter didn't answer the door. Perhaps he is dead.

Pandora! You are still on my mind, baby.

Saturday January 31st

It is nearly February and I have got nobody to send a Valentine's Day card to.

Sunday February 1st
FOURTH AFTER EPIPHANY

There was a lot of shouting downstairs late last night. The kitchen waste-bin* was knocked over and the back door kept being slammed. I wish my parents would be a bit more thoughtful. I have been through an emotional time and I need my sleep. Still I don't expect them to understand what it is like being in love. They have been married for fourteen-and-a-half years.

Went to Bert Baxter's this afternoon but thank God he has gone to Skegness* with the Evergreens. Sabre looked out of the living-room window. I gave him the "V" sign. I hope he doesn't remember.

commie *contempt.* a communist **hedge-clippers** *G.* Heckenschere **compensation** [ˌkɒmpenˈseɪʃn] *here: G.* Schadenersatz **to give a lecture** [ˈlektʃə] *G.* einen Vortrag halten **to make ends meet** *inf.* to manage to live on the little money you have **to be in a temper** to be very angry **betting-shop** a place where people bet money on horse races, etc. **waste-bin** a basket or other small container for paper you want to throw away **Skegness** name of a seaside town in East England

Monday February 2nd

PRESENTATION*

Mrs Lucas is back! I saw her pulling trees and bushes out of the earth and putting them in the back of a van, then she put all the gardening tools in and drove off. The van had "Women's Refuge*" painted on the side. Mr Lucas came over to our house to talk to my mother, I went down to say "hello" to him, but he was too upset to notice me. I asked my mother if she would get home early from work tonight, I'm fed up with waiting for my tea. She didn't.

Nigel got thrown out of school dinners today for swearing at* the toad-in-the-hole*, he said it was "all bleeding hole and no toad". I think Mrs Leech was quite right to throw him out, after all the first-years were present! We third-years must set an example. Pandora has got up a petition* to protest about the toad-in-the-hole. I will not sign it.

It was Good Samaritans today. So I was forced to go round to Bert Baxter's. I have missed the Algebra test! Ha! Ha! Ha! Bert gave me a stick of broken Skegness rock* and said he was sorry he rang the school to complain abut the hedge-clippers. He said he was lonely and wanted to hear a human voice. If I was the loneliest person in the world I wouldn't phone up our school. I would ring the speaking clock; that talks to you every ten seconds.

Tuesday February 3rd

My mother has not done any proper housework for days now. All she does is go to work, comfort Mr Lucas and read and smoke. The big-end* has gone on my father's car. I had to show him where to catch a bus into town. A man of forty not knowing where the bus stop is! My father looked such a scruff-bag* that I was ashamed* to be seen with him. I was glad when the bus came. I shouted through the window that he couldn't sit downstairs and smoke but he just waved and lit up a cigarette. There is a fifty pounds' fine* for doing that! If I was in charge of the buses I

presentation the day when people remember how Jesus as a boy was brought by his parents to the temple of Jerusalem (*G.* Mariä Lichtmess) **refuge** ['refju:dʒ] *here: G.* Zuflucht **Women's Refuge** a place where women can find help and refuge if they have been treated badly by their husbands **to swear (at)** *G.* verfluchen **toad-in-the-hole** *G.* in Pfannkuchenteig gebratene Wurst (the sausage is thought to look like a toad [*G.* Kröte] in a hole) **petition** [pə'tɪʃn] *G.* Bittschrift, Unterschriftenliste **rock** *here: G.* Zuckerstange **big-end** *cf. p. 17* **scruff-bag** *BE inf. contempt.* dirty and untidy person **to be ashamed** *G.* sich schämen **fine** sum of money you have to pay for breaking a law or a rule

would fine* smokers a thousand pounds *and* make them eat twenty Woodbines*.

My mother is reading *The Female Eunuch**, by Germaine Greer. My mother says it is the sort of book that changes your life. It hasn't changed mine, but I only glanced* through it. It is full of dirty words.

Wednesday February 4th
NEW MOON

I had my first wet dream*! So my mother was right about *The Female Eunuch*. It has changed my life.

The spot has got smaller.

Thursday February 5th

My mother has bought some of those overalls that painters and decorators wear. You can see her knickers* through them. I hope she doesn't wear them in the street.

She is having her ears pierced tomorrow. I think she is turning into a spendthrift*. Nigel's mother is a spendthrift. They are always getting letters about having their electricity cut off and all because Nigel's mother buys a pair of high heels every week.

I would like to know where the Family Allowance* goes, by rights it should be mine. I will ask my mother tomorrow.

Friday February 6th
THE QUEEN'S ACCESSION*, 1952

It is lousy having a working mother. She rushes in with big bags of shopping, cooks the tea then rushes around tarting herself up*. But she is still not doing any tidying up before comforting Mr Lucas. There has been a slice* of bacon between the cooker and the fridge for three days to my knowledge*!

to fine s.o. to make s.o. pay a fine **Woodbines** (trademark) name of cheap cigarettes **The Female Eunuch** ['ju:nək] a feminist book by Germaine Greer (1970) **to glance** [glɑ:ns] to look very quickly **wet dream** an erotic dream with orgasm **knickers** *BE inf. G.* Schlüpfer **spendthrift** *contempt.* s.o. who spends too much money **Family Allowance** a sum of money paid to families by the state **Queen's Accession** [æk'seʃn] *here:* the day when Elizabeth II became Queen of the United Kingdom **to tart o.s. up** *BE inf. contempt.* to make o.s. esp. attractive through make-up or clothes **slice** a thin, flat piece (e.g. of bread) **to my knowledge** as far as I know

I asked her about my Family Allowance today, she laughed and said she used it for buying gin and cigarettes. If the Social Services* hear about it she will get done!

Saturday February 7th

My mother and father have been shouting at each other non-stop for hours. It started because of the bacon down the side of the fridge and carried on into how much my father's car is costing to repair. I went up to my room and put my Abba records on. My father had the nerve to crash my door open and ask me to turn the volume down*. I did. When he got downstairs I turned it up again.

Nobody cooked any dinner so I went to the Chinese chip shop and bought a carton of chips and a sachet* of soy* sauce. I sat in the bus shelter and ate them, then walked about feeling sad. Came home. Fed dog. Read a bit of *Female Eunuch*. Felt a bit funny. Went to sleep.

Sunday February 8th
FIFTH AFTER EPIPHANY

My father came into my bedroom this morning, he said he wanted a chat. He looked at my Kevin Keegan* scrapbook*, screwed* the knob of my wardrobe door back on with his Swiss army knife, and asked me about school. Then he said he was sorry about yesterday and the shouting, he said my mother and him are "going through a bad patch*". He asked me if I had anything to say. I said he owed me thirty-two pence for the Chinese chips and soy sauce. He gave me a pound. So I made a profit of sixty-eight pence.

Social Services *BE* government services which are to help people with social and/or financial problems **to turn the volume down** *here:* to make the record player play less loud **sachet** ['sæʃeɪ] small plastic bag **soy** *G.* Soja **Kevin Keegan** famous British footballer **scrapbook** a book for collecting pictures, newspaper articles etc. **to screw** *G.* schrauben **to go through a bad patch** *BE fig.* to have difficulties

Monday February 9th

There was a removal lorry* outside Mr Lucas's house this morning. Mrs Lucas and some other women were carrying furniture from the house and stacking* it on the pavement. Mr Lucas was looking out from his bedroom window. He looked a bit frightened. Mrs Lucas was laughing and pointing up to Mr Lucas and all the other women started laughing and singing "Why was he born so beautiful?"

My mother phoned Mr Lucas up and asked him if he was all right. Mr Lucas said he wasn't going to work today because he had to guard* the stereo and records from his wife. My father helped Mrs Lucas put the gas stove* in the removal van, then he and my mother walked to the bus stop together. I walked behind them because my mother was wearing long dangly earrings and my father's trouser turn-ups* had come down. They started to quarrel about something so I crossed over the road and went to school the long way round.

Bert Baxter was OK today. He told me about the First World War*. He said his life was saved by a Bible he always carried in his breast pocket. He showed me the Bible, it was printed in 1956. I think Bert is going a bit senile*.

Pandora! The memory of you is a constant torment!

Tuesday February 10th

Mr Lucas is staying with us until he gets some new furniture.

My father has gone to Matlock* to try to sell electric storage heaters* to a big hotel.

Our gas boiler has packed in*. It is freezing cold.

removal lorry a lorry in which people put their furniture when they move from one house to another **to stack** to pile up (*G.* aufstapeln) **to guard** [gɑːd] to protect and keep from danger **stove** [stəʊv] *G.* Herd **turn-up** *BE* the turned-up part at the bottom of some trouser legs **First World War** (1914–1918) also called: the Great War **to go senile** ['siːnaɪl] to become confused and helpless because of being old **Matlock** a town in Derbyshire (Northern England) **electric storage heater** *G.* Nachtspeicherofen **to pack in** *BE inf.* to stop working

Wednesday February 11th
FIRST QUARTER

My father rang up from Matlock to say he has lost his Barclaycard* and can't get home tonight, so Mr Lucas and my mother were up all night trying to mend* the boiler. I went down at ten o'clock to see if I could help but the kitchen door was jammed*. Mr Lucas said he couldn't open it just at that moment because he was at a crucial* stage* with the boiler and my mother was helping him and she had her hands full.

Thursday February 12th
LINCOLN'S* BIRTHDAY

I found my mother dyeing* her hair in the bathroom tonight. This has come as a complete shock to me. For thirteen and three-quarter years I have thought I had a mother with red hair, now I find out that it is really light brown. My mother asked me not to tell my father. What a state their marriage must be in! I wonder if my father knows that she wears a padded* bra*? She doesn't hang them on the line to dry, but I have seen them shoved* down the side of the airing cupboard*. I wonder what other secrets my mother has got?

Friday February 13th

It was an unlucky day for me all right!

Pandora doesn't sit next to me in Geography any more. Barry Kent does. He kept copying my work and blowing bubblegum in my ears. I told Miss Elf but she is scared of* Barry Kent as well, so she didn't say anything to him.

Pandora looked luscious* today, she was wearing a split skirt which showed her legs. She has got a scab* on one of her knees. She was wearing Nigel's football scarf round her wrist*, but Miss Elf saw it and told her to take it off. Miss Elf is not scared of Pandora. I have sent her a Valentine's Day card (Pandora, not Miss Elf).

Barclaycard a credit card of Barclay's, a large British bank **to mend** to repair **to jam** to block **crucial** ['kru:ʃl] very important **stage** [steɪdʒ] *G.* Phase, Abschnitt **Abraham Lincoln** (1809–1865), a US president **to dye** [daɪ] to give a different colour to **padded** *G.* wattiert, gepolstert **bra** [brɑ:] *G.* Büstenhalter **to shove** to push violently or without care **airing cupboard** *BE G.* Wäschetrockenschrank **to be scared of** to be very afraid of **luscious** ['lʌʃəs] sexually extremely attractive **scab** [skæb] *G.* Schorf **wrist** *G.* Handgelenk

Science*—made apple crumble*. Came home. Vacuumed hall, lounge*, and breakfast room. Peeled* potatoes, chopped* up cabbage*, cut finger, rinsed* blood off cabbage. Put chops under grill, looked in cookery book for a recipe* for gravy. Made gravy. Strained* lumps out with a colander*. Set table, served dinner, washed up. Put burnt saucepans in to soak*. Got washing out of machine; everything blue, including white underwear and handkerchiefs. Hung washing on clothes-horse*. Fed dog. Ironed PE kit*, cleaned shoes. Did homework. Took dog for a walk, had bath. Cleaned bath. Made three cups of tea. Washed cups up. Went to bed. Just my luck to have an assertive mother!

Tuesday March 10th
PRINCE EDWARD* BORN, 1964

Why couldn't I have been born Prince Edward and Prince Edward been born Adrian Mole? I am treated like a serf*.

Wednesday March 11th

Dragged* myself to school after doing paper round and housework. My mother wouldn't give me a note excusing me from Games so I left my PE kit at home. I just couldn't face running about in the cold wind.

That sadist Mr Jones made me run all the way home to fetch my PE kit. The dog must have followed me out of the house because when I got to the school gate it was there before me. I tried to shut the dog out but it squeezed* through the railings* and followed me into the playground. I ran into the changing rooms and left the dog outside but I could hear its loud bark echoing around the school. I tried to sneak* into the playing fields but the dog saw me and followed behind, then it saw the football and joined in the lesson! The dog is dead good at football, even Mr Jones was laughing until the dog punctured* the ball.

Mr Scruton, the pop-eyed* headmaster, saw everything from his win-

Domestic Science a subject at school in which pupils are taught how to cook, etc. **apple crumble** *G.* mit Streuseln überbackenes Apfeldessert **lounge** [laʊndʒ] *BE* living room **to peel** to take the skin off a fruit **to chop up** to cut into small pieces **cabbage** ['kæbɪdʒ] *G.* Kohl **to rinse** [rɪns] to wash lightly with clean water **recipe** ['resɪpɪ] *G.* Kochrezept **to strain** *here: G.* (durch)sieben **colander** ['kʌləndə] *G.* Sieb **to soak** [səʊk] to make very wet **clothes-horse** *G.* Wäscheständer **PE kit** clothes needed for the PE (= Physical Education) lesson **Prince Edward** a son of Elizabeth II **serf** [sɜːf] *arch.* a slave **to drag** to pull with difficulty **to squeeze** to press very tightly **railings** *here:* metal fence **to sneak** to move quietly so that one is neither seen nor heard **to puncture** ['pʌŋktʃə] to make a small hole into **pop-eyed** *inf.* with eyes which are wide open

Saturday February 14th
ST VALENTINE'S DAY*

I only got one Valentine's Day card. It was in my mother's handwriting so it doesn't count. My mother had a massive card delivered, it was so big that a GPO* van had to bring it to the door. She went all red when she opened the envelope and saw the card. It was dead good. There was a big satin* elephant holding a bunch* of plastic flowers in its trunk* and a bubble* coming out of its mouth saying "Hi, Honey Bun! I ain't* never gonna* forget you!" There was no name written inside, just drawings of hearts with "Pauline" written inside them. My father's card was very small and had a bunch of purple flowers on the front. My father had written on the inside "Let's try again".

Here is the poem I wrote inside Pandora's card.

Pandora!
I adore* ya*.
I implore* ye.
Don't ignore me.

I wrote it left-handed so that she wouldn't know it was from me.

Sunday February 15th
SEPTUAGESIMA*

Mr Lucas moved back to his empty house last night. I expect he got fed up with all the rowing* over the elephant Valentine's Day card. I told my father that my mother can't help it if a man secretly admires her. My father gave a nasty laugh and said "You've got a lot to learn, son".

I cleared off* to my grandma's at dinner-time. She cooked me a proper Sunday dinner with gravy* and individual Yorkshire puddings*. She is never too busy to make real custard* either.

St. Valentine's Day on this day people send a person they love an anonymous greeting card **GPO** *BE short for:* General Post Office, the British postal service **satin** ['sætɪn] *G.* samtig, Satin- **a bunch of** a number of **trunk** *here: G.* Rüssel **bubble** *here: G.* Sprechblase **ain't** *sl.* [eɪnt] *here:* am not **gonna** *inf., esp. AE* going to **to adore** [ə'dɔː] to love very much (like a god or goddess) **ya/ye** *arch.* you **to implore** [ɪm'plɔː] to ask on one's knees **Septuagesima** [ˌseptjʊə'dʒesɪmə] the third Sunday before Lent (lent *G.* Fastenzeit) **rowing** *here:* noisy quarrelling **to clear off** *inf.* to leave quickly **gravy** ['greɪvɪ] *G.* Soße **Yorkshire pudding** *BE* a warm baked mixture of flour, milk and eggs, often eaten with roast beef **custard** ['kʌstəd] *G.* Vanillesoße

I took the dog with me and we all went for a walk in the afternoon to settle* our dinners.

My grandma hasn't spoken to my mother since the row about the cardigans. Grandma says she "won't set foot in that house again!" Grandma asked me if I believed in life after death. I said I didn't and grandma told me that she had joined the Spiritualist* church and has heard my grandad talking about his rhubarb*. My grandad has been dead for four years!!! She is going on Wednesday night to try to get in touch with him again and she wants me to go with her. She says I have got an aura* around me.

The dog choked on a chicken bone but we held it upside down and banged it hard, and the bone fell out. I've left the dog at grandma's to recover from its ordeal*.

Looked up "Septuagesima" in my pocket dictionary. It didn't have it. Will look in the school dictionary, tomorrow.

Lay awake for ages thinking about God, Life and Death and Pandora.

Monday February 16th
WASHINGTON'S BIRTHDAY OBSERVANCE*

A letter from the BBC!!!!! A white oblong* envelope with BBC in red fat letters. My name and address on the front! Could it be that they wanted my poems? Alas*, no. But a letter from a bloke* called John Tydeman, here is what he wrote:

> Dear Adrian Mole,
>
> Thank you for the poems which you sent to the BBC and which somehow landed up on my desk. I read them with interest and, taking into account your tender* years, I must confess that they do show some promise. However they are not of sufficient quality for us to consider including them in any of our current* poetry programmes. Have you thought of offering them to your School Magazine or to your local Parish* Magazine? (If you have one.)

to settle *here: G.* verdauen **Spiritualist** believing that the dead can talk to people who are still alive **rhubarb** ['ruːbɑːb] *G.* Rhabarber **aura** ['ɔːrə] *G.* Ausstrahlung **ordeal** [ɔː'diːl] extremely difficult and unpleasant situation **Washington's Birthday Observance** George Washington (1732–1799), whose birthday is a national holiday in the USA, was the first US president **oblong** *G.* rechteckig **alas** *arch.* [ə'læs] unfortunately **bloke** *BE inf.* a man **tender** *here:* young, without experience **current** *G.* aktuell **Parish** *G.* Pfarr-, Pfarrei

If, in future, you wish to submit* any of your work to the BBC may I suggest you get it typed out and retain*, also, a copy for yourself. The BBC does not normally consider submissions in handwritten manuscript form and, despite the neatness of presentation, I did have some difficulty in making out *all* of the words—particularly at the end of one poem entitled "The Tap" where there was a rather nasty blotch* which had caused the ink to run. (A teastain* or a tear-stain? A case of "Your Tap runneth* over"!)

Since you wish to follow a literary career I suggest you will need to develop a thick skin in order to accept many of the inevitable* future rejections* you may receive with good grace* and the minimum of personal pain.

With my best wishes to you for future literary efforts—and, above all, Good Luck!

Yours sincerely,
John Tydeman

P.S. I enclose a poem by a certain John Mole which appeared in this week's *Times Literary Supplement**. Is he a relation? It is very good.

My mother and father were really impressed. I kept getting it out and reading it at school. I was hoping one of the teachers would ask to read it but none of them did.

Bert Baxter read it while I was doing the rotten washing up. He said they were "all a load of drug addicts* in the BBC"! His brother-in-law's uncle once lived next door to a tea lady at Broadcasting House*, so Bert knows all about the BBC.

Pandora got seventeen Valentine's Day cards. Nigel got seven. Even Barry Kent whom everybody hates got three! I just smiled when everybody asked me how many I got. Anyway I bet I am the only person in the school to get a letter from the BBC.

Tuesday February 17th

Barry Kent said he would do me over* unless I gave him twenty-five pence every day. I told him that he was wasting his time demanding*

to submit to to send to **to retain** to keep **blotch** *G.* Klecks **stain** *G.* Fleck **runneth** *arch.* runs **inevitable** [ɪnˈevɪtəbl] unavoidable **rejection** [rɪˈdʒekʃn] not accepting **with good grace** willingly, cheerfully **Times Literary Supplement** (TLS) an important weekly newspaper with articles about new books **drug addict** s.o. who cannot live without drugs **Broadcasting House** central office of the BBC in London **to do s.o. over** *inf.* to hurt s.o. badly **to demand** *G.* verlangen, fordern

money with menaces* from me. I never have any spare money. My mother puts my pocket money straight into my building-society* account* and gives me fifteen pence a day for a Mars bar*. Barry Kent said I would have to give him my dinner money! I told him that my father pays it by cheque since it went up to sixty pence a day, but Barry Kent hit me in the goolies* and walked off saying "There's more where that came from".

I have put my name down for a paper round.

Wednesday February 18th

FULL MOON

Woke up with a pain in my goolies. Told my mother. She wanted to look but I didn't want her to so she said I would have to soldier* on. She wouldn't give me a note excusing me from Games, so I had to stumble* around in the mud again. Barry Kent trod on my head in the scrum*. Mr Jones saw him and sent him off for an early shower.

I wish I could have a non-painful illness so I could be excused Games. Something like a weak heart would be all right.

Fetched the dog from grandma's, she has given it a shampoo and set*. It smells like the perfume counter in Woolworth's.

I went to the Spiritualist meeting with my grandma, it was full of dead old people. One madman stood up and said he had a radio inside his head which told him what to do. Nobody took any notice of him, so he sat down again. A woman called Alice Tonks started grunting* and rolling her eyes about and talking to somebody called Arthur Mayfield, but my grandad kept quiet. My grandma was a bit sad so when we got home I made her a cup of Horlicks*. She gave me fifty pence and I walked home with the dog.

Started reading *Animal Farm**, by George Orwell. I think I might like to be a vet when I grow up.

menace ['menəs] *G.* (Be-)Drohung **building society** *G.* (Bau-)Sparkasse **account** *G.* Konto **bar** a long piece (e.g. of chocolate) **goolies** *sl.* male genitals **to soldier on** to go on working hard even under bad conditions **to stumble** (to start) to fall over **scrum** a group of rugby players who push against each other with their heads down, trying to get the ball **set** *here: G.* Festiger **to grunt** to make a rough noise (like a pig) **Horlicks** (trademark) name of a malted milk drink **Animal Farm** a novel by George Orwell (1903–1950) about the revolution of animals on a farm and its results: a pig becomes the absolute dictator of the farm.

Thursday February 19th

PRINCE ANDREW* BORN, 1960

It's all right for Prince Andrew, he is protected by bodyguards. He doesn't have Barry Kent nicking* money off him. Fifty pence gone just like that! I wish I knew karate, I would chop* Barry Kent in his windpipe*.

It is quiet at home, my parents are not speaking to each other.

Friday February 20th

Barry Kent told Miss Elf to "get stuffed*" in Geography today so she sent him to Mr Scruton to be punished*. I hope he gets fifty lashes*. I am going to make friends with Craig Thomas. He is one of the biggest third-years*. I bought him a Mars bar in break today. I pretended I felt sick and didn't feel like eating it myself. He said, "Ta* Moley". That is the first time he has spoken to me. If I play my cards right I could be in his gang. Then Barry Kent wouldn't dare touch me again.

My mother is reading another sex book, it is called *The Second Sex**, by a frog* writer called Simone De Beauvoir*. She left it on the coffee table in the living room where anybody could have seen it, even my grandma!

Saturday February 21st

Had a dead good dream that Sabre was brutally savaging* Barry Kent. Mr Scruton and Miss Elf were watching. Pandora was there, she was wearing her split skirt. She put her arms round me and said, "I am of the second sex". Then I woke up to find I had had my second W.D.* I have to put my pyjamas in the washing machine so my mother doesn't find out.

Had a good look at my face in the bathroom mirror today. I have got five spots as well as the one on my chin. I have got a few hairs on my lip. It looks as if I shall have to start shaving soon.

Prince Andrew a son of Queen Elizabeth II **to nick** *inf.* to steal **to chop** to hit quickly by moving one's hand downward **windpipe** *G.* Luftröhre **get stuffed!** *BE sl.* go away! **to punish** *G.* bestrafen **lash** *G.* Peitschenhieb **third-year** a pupil in his/her third year at a secondary school **ta** [tɑː] *BE inf.* thank you **The Second Sex** (sex *G.* Geschlecht) a feminist book by the French writer **Simone de Beauvoir**, published in 1949 **frog** *inf. contempt.* French **to savage** ['sævɪdʒ] to attack wildly **W.D.** *short for:* wet dream *(cf. p. 22)*

Went to the garage with my father, he expected to get the car back today but it still isn't ready. All the bits are on the work-bench. My father's eyes filled up with tears. I was ashamed of him. We walked to Sainsbury's*. My father bought tins of salmon*, crab and shrimps* and a black forest cake and some dead yukky white cheese covered in grape pips*. My mother was dead mad at him when we got home because he had forgotten the bread, butter and toilet paper. She says he can't be trusted to go on his own again. My father cheered up a bit.

Sunday February 22nd
SEXAGESIMA*

My father has gone fishing with the dog. Mr Lucas came for dinner and stayed for tea. He ate three slices of the black forest cake. We played Monopoly. Mr Lucas was banker. My mother kept going into jail. I won because I was the only one concentrating properly. My father came in the front door and Mr Lucas went out of the back door. My father said he had been looking forward to the black forest cake all day. There was none left. My father said he had not had a bite to eat or a bite on his fishing line all day. My mother gave him grape-pip cheese on Ry-king* for his supper. He threw it at the wall and said he wasn't a ****** mouse he was a ****** man and my mother said it was a long time since he had done any ******! I was sent out of the room then. It is a terrible thing to hear your own mother swearing. I blame it on all those books she has been reading. She hasn't ironed* my school uniform yet, I hope she remembers.

I let the dog sleep in my room tonight, it doesn't like quarrelling.

Sainsbury's name of some quality supermarkets in Britain **salmon** ['sæmən] *G.* Lachs **shrimp** *G.* Garnele **grape pip** *G.* Traubenkern **Sexagesima** [ˌseksəˈdʒesɪmə] the second Sunday before Lent (lent *G.* Fastenzeit) **Ry-king** (trademark) name for some rye (*G.* Roggen) bread **to iron** ['aɪən] *G.* bügeln

Monday February 23rd

Got a letter from Mr Cherry the newsagent to say I can start a paper round tomorrow. Worse luck!

Bert Baxter is worried about Sabre because he is off* his food and not trying to bite anybody. He asked me to take him to the PDSA* for a check-up. I said I would take him tomorrow if his condition hadn't improved.

I'm fed up with washing up for Bert. He seems to live off fried eggs, it is no joke trying to wash up in cold water without any washing-up liquid. Also there is never a dry tea towel. In fact there are never any tea towels and Sabre has ripped up all the bath towels so I don't know how Bert can even have a wash! I think I'll see if I can get Bert a home help.

I have got to concentrate on getting my GCEs* if I want to be a vet.

Tuesday February 24th

ST MATTHIAS

Got up at six o'clock for my paper round. I have got Elm Tree Avenue. It is dead posh*. All the papers they read are very heavy: *The Times*, the *Daily Telegraph* and the *Guardian**. Just my luck!

Bert said Sabre is better, he tried to bite the milkman.

Wednesday February 25th

Bed early tonight because of my paper round. Delivered twenty-five *Punches** as well as the papers.

Thursday February 26th

The papers got mixed up today. Elm Tree Avenue got the *Sun** and the *Mirror** and Corporation Row got the heavy papers.

I don't know why everybody went so mad. You'd think they would enjoy reading a different paper for a change.

to be off s.th. *inf.* not to like s.th. any longer **PDSA** (*short for:* People's Dispensary for Sick Animals) an organzation that helps sick animals **GCE** (*short for:* General Certificate of Education) *here:* O-level examinations taken at the age of 15 or 16 (after 1988 called GCSE) **posh** *coll.* elegant, upper-class, rich **The Times, The Daily Telegraph, The Guardian** daily quality newspapers in Britain **Punch** a monthly satirical magazine in Britain (first published in 1841!) **The Sun, The Daily Mirror** cheap popular daily newspapers, mainly interested in sport and sensational news

Friday February 27th
LAST QUARTER

Early this morning I saw Pandora walking down the drive* of 69 Elm Tree Avenue. She had a riding hat and jodhpurs* on so she couldn't have been on her way to school. I didn't let her see me. I don't want her to know that I am doing a menial* job.

So now I know where Pandora lives! I had a good look at the house. It is much bigger than ours. It has got rolled-up wooden blinds* at all the windows, and the rooms look like jungles because of all the green plants. I looked through the letterbox and saw the big ginger* cat eating something on the kitchen table. They have the *Guardian*, *Punch*, *Private Eye**, and *New Society**. Pandora reads *Jackie*, the comic for girls; she is not an intellectual, like me. But I don't suppose Malcolm Muggeridge's wife is either.

Saturday February 28th

Pandora has got a little fat horse called "Blossom". She feeds it and makes it jump over barrels* every morning before school. I know because I hid behind her father's Volvo and then followed her to a field next to the disused railway line. I hid behind a scrap* car in the corner of the field and watched her. She looked dead good in her riding stuff, her chest was wobbling like mad. She will need to wear a bra soon. My heart was beating so loudly in my throat that I felt like a stereo loudspeaker, so I left before she heard me.

People complained because the papers were late. I had a *Guardian* left over in my paper bag so I took it home to read. It was full of spelling mistakes. It is disgusting when you think of how many people who can spell are out of work.

drive *here: G.* Einfahrt **jodhpurs** ['dʒɒdpəz] trousers used when riding horses **menial** ['miːnjəl] *here:* boring, tiring **blind** *G.* Rollo, Rollladen **ginger** orange-brown **Private Eye** a British monthly satirical magazine, more political than Punch **New Society** a British monthly political magazine **barrel** *G.* Fass **scrap** *here: G.* Schrott

Sunday March 1st

QUINQUAGESIMA*. ST DAVID'S DAY

I took some sugar to Blossom before I did my paper round. It brought me closer to Pandora somehow.

Have strained* my back because of carrying all the Sunday supplements. Took the leftover *Sunday People** home as a present to my mother but she said it was only fit for lining* the dustbin. Got my two pounds and six pence for six mornings, it is slave labour*! *And* I have to give Barry Kent half of it. Mr Cherry said he had a complaint from number 69 Elm Tree Avenue, that they didn't get a *Guardian* yesterday. Mr Cherry sent a *Daily Express** round with his apologies*, but Pandora's father brought it back to the shop and said he "would rather go without*".

Didn't bother reading the papers today, I am fed up with papers. Had chow mein* and beansprouts* for Sunday dinner.

Mr Lucas came round when my father had gone to visit grandma. He was wearing a plastic daffodil* in his sports jacket.

My spots have completely gone. It must be the early morning air.

Monday March 2nd

My mother has just come into my room and said she had something awful to tell me. I sat up in bed and put a dead serious expression on my face just in case she'd got six months to live or she'd been caught shoplifting or something. She fiddled* with the curtains, dropped cigarette ash all over my Concorde model and started mumbling on about "adult relationships" and "life being complicated" and how she must "find herself". She said she was fond of me. Fond!!! And would hate to hurt me. And then she said that for some women marriage was like being in prison. Then she went out.

Marriage is nothing like being in prison! Women are let out every day to go to the shops and stuff, and quite a lot go to work. I think my mother is being a bit melodramatic.

Quinquagesima [ˌkwɪŋkwəˈdʒesɪmə] the Sunday before Ash Wednesday **to strain** to hurt a part of one's body by using it too much **Sunday People** a British popular Sunday newspaper **to line** *here: G.* auslegen, ausschlagen **slave** [sleɪv] a person who is not free and must work for his/her "owner" **labour** [ˈleɪbə] very hard work **The Daily Express** a popular daily newspaper in Britain **apology** [əˈpɒlədʒɪ] a statement that one feels sorry for having done s. th. **to go without** *here:* to live without **chow mein** [ˈtʃaʊ ˈmeɪn] Chinese-American dish: mushrooms, shrimps, etc. with fried noodles **beansprout** [ˈbiːnspraʊt] *G.* Sojabohnenkeim **daffodil** *G.* Osterglocke, Narzisse **to fiddle** to nervously touch s. th. with one's fingers

Finished *Animal Farm*. It is dead symbolic. I cried when Boxer* was taken to the vet's. From now on I shall treat pigs with the contempt* they deserve*. I am boycotting pork* of all kinds.

Tuesday March 3rd
SHROVE TUESDAY*

I gave Barry Kent his protection money today. I don't see how there can be a God. If there was surely he wouldn't let people like Barry Kent walk about menacing intellectuals? Why are bigger youths unpleasant to smaller youths? Perhaps their brains are easily worn out with all the extra work they have to do making bigger bones and stuff, or it could be that the big youths have got brain damage because of all the sport they play, or perhaps big youths just *like* menacing and fighting. When I go to university I may study the problem.

I will have my thesis* published and I will send a copy to Barry Kent. Perhaps by then he will have learnt to read.

My mother had forgotten that today was pancake day. I reminded her at 11 p.m. I'm sure she burnt them deliberately. I will be fourteen in one month's time.

Wednesday March 4th
ASH WEDNESDAY

Had a nasty shock this morning. Took my empty paper sack back to Mr Cherry's newsagent's and saw Mr Lucas looking at those magazines on the top shelf. I stood behind the Mills and Boon* rack and distinctly* saw him choose *Big and Bouncy**, pay for it and leave the shop with it hidden inside his coat. *Big and Bouncy* is extremely indecent*. It is full of disgusting pictures. My mother should be informed.

Boxer name of a very old horse in Orwell's novel (*cf. p. 29*), – one of the nice characters, but in the end sold to a butcher by the pigs who have taken over the "government" of the farm **contempt** [–'–] *G.* Verachtung **to deserve s.th.** to have a right to s.th. **pork** meat from a pig **Shrove Tuesday** (also called: Pancake Day) on this day before Ash Wednesday it is traditional to eat pancakes in Britain **thesis** ['θiːsɪz] *here: G.* Diplomarbeit, Doktorarbeit **Mills and Boon** publishers of love stories **distinctly** clearly **bouncy** *here:* not flat; jumping up and down **indecent** [ɪn'diːsnt] not proper; embarrassing

Thursday March 5th

My father got his car back from the garage today. He was cleaning it and gloating over* it for a whole two hours. I noticed that the stick-on waving hand I bought him for Christmas was missing from the rear window. I told him he ought to complain to the garage but he said he didn't want to make a fuss*. We went to my grandma's to test-drive the car. She gave us a cup of Bovril* and a piece of yukky seedcake. She didn't ask how my mother was, she said my father was looking thin and pale and needed "feeding up".

She told me that Bert Baxter had been thrown out of the Evergreens because of his bad behaviour at Skegness. The coach was waiting for two hours for him at the coach station. A search party* was sent out to look in the pubs, then Bert came back, drunk but alone and another search party was sent out to look for the first search party. In the end the police had to be sent for and they took hours to round up* all the pensioners and get them in the coach.

My grandma said the journey back was a nightmare*. All the pensioners kept falling out* (with each other not out of the coach). Bert Baxter was reciting* a dirty poem about an Eskimo and Mrs Harriman had a funny turn* and had to have her corsets loosened.

Grandma said two pensioners had passed on* since the outing*, she blamed Bert Baxter and said "He as good as murdered them", but I think it was more likely that the cold wind at Skegness killed them off. I said, "Bert Baxter is not so bad when you get to know him". She said she didn't understand why the Good Lord took my grandad and left scum* like Baxter. Then she pulled her lips tight and dabbled* her eyes with a handkerchief, so we left.

My mother was out when we got home, she has joined some women's group.

Heard my father say "goodnight" to the car. He must be cracking up*!

to gloat over *contempt.* to show very great pleasure at **to make a fuss** *inf. here: G.* Aufhebens machen **Bovril** (trademark) *G.* Rinderextrakt **search party** a group of people looking for s.o. or s.th. **to round up** to bring together **nightmare** ['naɪtmeə] a terrible and frightening dream **to fall out with** to quarrel with **to recite** to say s.th. aloud from memory **to have a funny turn** *inf.* to become ill suddenly **to pass on** *inf.* to die **outing** pleasure trip **scum** *inf. contempt.* extremely bad person **to dabble** to touch s.th. quickly, trying to clean it **to crack up** *inf.* to become mad

Friday March 6th
NEW MOON

Mr Cherry is very pleased with my work and he has raised* my wages* by two and a half pence an hour. He also offered me the Corporation Row evening round, but I declined his offer. Corporation Row is where the council* put all the bad tenants*. Barry Kent lives at number 13.

Mr Cherry gave me two back copies of *Big and Bouncy.* He told me not to tell my mother. As if I would! I have put them under my mattress. Intellectuals like me are allowed to be interested in sex. It is ordinary people like Mr Lucas who should be ashamed of themselves.

Phoned Social Services today and asked about a home help for Bert Baxter. I told a lie and said I was his grandson. They are sending a social worker to see him on Monday.

Used my father's library tickets to get *War and Peace** out. I have lost my own.

Took dog to meet Blossom. They got on well.

Saturday March 7th

After paper round went back to bed and stayed there all morning reading *Big and Bouncy. Felt* like I have never *felt* before.

Went to Sainsbury's with my mother and father but the women in there reminded me of *Big and Bouncy*, even the ones over thirty! My mother said I looked hot and bothered* and sent me back to the multi-storey* car park to keep the dog company.

The dog already had company, it was barking and whining* so loudly that a crowd of people were standing around saying "the poor thing" and "how cruel to leave it tied up in such a fashion". The dog had twisted its collar* on the gear lever* and its eyes were bulging out* of its head. When it saw me it tried to jump up and nearly killed itself.

I tried to explain to the people that I was going to be a vet when I grew up, but they wouldn't listen and started to say things about the RSPCA*.

to raise *here:* to make bigger **wages** ['weɪdʒɪz] weekly payment for work **council** *BE G.* Stadtrat, Stadtverwaltung **tenant** s. o. who pays money for the use of an apartment or a house **War and Peace** a novel by the Russian author Tolstoy (1828–1910) about life in Russia during the war against Napoleon **bothered** worried **multi-storey** having several floors **to whine** [waɪn] *G.* jaulen, heulen **collar** ['kɒlə] *here:* a leather band round a dog's neck **gear lever** ['gɪəˌliːvə] *G.* (beim Auto:) Schaltknüppel **to bulge out** *here: G.* heraustreten **RSPCA** *cf. p. 5*

The car was locked so I was forced to break the little window open and unlock the door by putting my hand through. The dog went mad with joy when I untangled him, so the people went away. But my father didn't go mad with joy when he saw the damage, he went mad with rage*. He threw the Sainsbury's bags down, broke the eggs, squashed the cakes and drove home too fast. Nobody said anything on the way home, and only the dog was smiling.

Finished *War and Peace*. It was quite good.

Sunday March 8th
FIRST IN LENT

My mother has gone to a woman's workshop on assertiveness* training. Men aren't allowed. I asked my father what "assertiveness training" is. He said "God knows, but whatever it is, it's bad news for me".

We had boil-in-the-bag cod* in butter sauce and oven-cooked chips for Sunday dinner, followed by tinned peaches and Dream-topping*. My father opened a bottle of white wine and let me have some. I don't know much about wine but it seemed a pleasant enough vintage*. We watched a film on television, then my mother came home and started bossing us around*. She said, "The worm has turned", and "Things are going to be different around here", and things like that. Then she went into the kitchen and started making a chart* dividing all the housework into three. I pointed out to her that I already had a paper round to do, an old age pensioner to look after and a dog to feed, as well as my school work, but she didn't listen, she put the chart on the wall and said "We start tomorrow".

Monday March 9th
COMMONWEALTH DAY*

Cleaned toilet, washed basin and bath before doing my paper round. Came home, made breakfast, put washing in machine, went to school. Gave Barry Kent his menaces money, went to Bert Baxter's, waited for social worker who didn't come, had school dinner. Had Domestic

rage great anger **assertiveness** [ə'sɜːtɪvnɪs] *here: G.* Bestimmtheit, Selbstbehauptung **cod** *G.* Kabeljau **topping** cream or cheese that is poured on top of other food **vintage** ['vɪntɪdʒ] *G.* (beim Wein:) Jahrgang **to boss s.o. around** *contempt.* to keep telling s.o. what to do **chart** list, plan **Commonwealth (of Nations)** a large group of countries all over the world that were once a part of the British Empire and still accept the Queen as their official head of state

dow. He ordered me to take the dog home. I told him I would miss my sitting for school dinners but he said it would teach me not to bring pets to school.

Mrs Leech, the kitchen supervisor*, did a very kind thing. She put my curry and rice, spotted dick* and custard into the oven to keep warm. Mrs Leech doesn't like Mr Scruton so she gave me a large marrow-bone* to take home for the dog.

Thursday March 12th

Woke up this morning to find my face covered in huge red spots. My mother said they were caused by nerves but I am still convinced that my diet is inadequate. We have been eating a lot of boil-in-the-bag stuff* lately. Perhaps I am allergic to plastic. My mother rang Dr Gray's receptionist to make an appointment, but the earliest he can see me is next Monday! For all he knows I could have lassa fever* and be spreading* it all around the district! I told my mother to say that I was an emergency case but she said I was "over-reacting as usual". She said a few spots didn't mean I was dying. I couldn't believe it when she said she was going to work as usual. Surely her child should come before her job?

I rang my grandma and she came round in a taxi and took me to her house and put me to bed. I am there now. It is very clean and peaceful. I am wearing my dead grandad's pyjamas. I have just had a bowl of barley* and beef soup. It is my first proper nourishment* for weeks.

I expect there will be a row when my mother comes home and finds that I have gone. But frankly*, my dear diary, I don't give a damn.

Friday March 13th
MOON'S FIRST QUARTER*

The emergency doctor came to my grandma's last night at 11.30 p.m. He diagnosed that I am suffering from *acne vulgaris*. He said it was so common that it is regarded as a normal state of adolescence*. He thought it was higly unlikely* that I have got lassa fever because I have not been to Africa this year. He told grandma to take the disinfected sheets off the

supervisor a person who is in charge of s.th. **spotted dick** *BE G.* Kochpudding mit Rosinen **marrow-bone** *G.* Markknochen **stuff** *inf.* things (*G.* Zeug) **lassa fever** serious disease (found in West Africa) **to spread** *G.* verbreiten **barley** *G.* Gerste **nourishment** ['nʌrɪʃmənt] food **frank** honest **moon's first quarter** the time when half of the moon can be seen from Earth **adolescence** [ˌædəʊ'lesns] period when people are between 13 and 16 years old **unlikely** *G.* unwahrscheinlich

doors and windows. Grandma said she would like a second opinion. That was when the doctor lost his temper. He shouted in a very loud voice, "The lad has only got a few teenage spots, for Christ's sake*!"

Grandma said she would complain to the Medical Council but the doctor just laughed and went downstairs and slammed the door. My father came round before he went to work and brought my Social Studies homework and the dog. He said that if I was not out of bed when he got home at lunchtime he would thrash* me to within an inch of my life*.

He took my grandma into the kitchen and had a loud talk with her. I heard him saying, "Things are very bad between me and Pauline, and all we are arguing over now is who *doesn't* get custody* of Adrian". Surely my father made a mistake. He must have meant who *did* get custody of me.

So the worst has happened, my skin has gone to pot* and my parents are splitting up.

Saturday March 14th

It is official. They are getting a divorce! Neither of them wants to leave the house so the spare* room is being turned into a bedsitter for my father. This could have a very bad effect on me. It could prevent me from being a vet.

My mother gave me five pounds this morning and told me not to tell my father. I bought some bio-spot cream for my skin and the new Abba LP.

I rang Mr Cherry and said I had personal problems and would be unable to work for a few weeks. Mr Cherry said that he knew that my parents were divorcing because my father had cancelled* my mother's *Cosmopolitan**.

My father gave me five pounds and told me not to tell my mother. I spent some of it on buying some purple paper and envelopes so that the BBC will be impressed and read my poems. The rest of it will have to go on Barry Kent and his menaces money. I don't think anybody in the world can be as unhappy as me. If I didn't have my poetry I would be a raving loonie* by now.

for Christ's sake (an expression showing that s.o. is angry) **to thrash s.o.** to hit s.o. very hard **within in an inch of s.o.'s life** *inf.* almost to death **custody** ['kʌstədɪ] *G.* Fürsorgerecht **to go to pot** *inf.* to become ruined **divorce** official ending of a marriage **spare** *here:* extra **to cancel** *here: G.* abbestellen **Cosmopolitan** [ˌkɒzmə'pɒlɪtən] name of a monthly women's magazine **raving loonie** ['reɪvɪŋ 'lu:nɪ] *sl.* wild and mad person

Went out for a sad walk and took Pandora's horse two pounds of cooking apples. Thought of a poem about Blossom. Wrote it down when I got back to the house where I live.

Blossom, by Adrian Mole, aged nearly fourteen

Little Brown Horse
Eating apples in a field,
Perhaps one day
My heart will be healed.
I stroke the places Pandora has sat
Wearing her jodhpurs and riding hat.
Goodbye, brown horse.
I turn and retreat,
The rain and mud are wetting my feet.

I have sent it to the BBC. I marked the envelope "Urgent*".

Sunday March 15th
SECOND IN LENT

The house is very quiet. My father sits in the spare room smoking and my mother sits in the bedroom smoking. They are not eating much.

Mr Lucas has phoned my mother three times. All she says to him is "not yet, it's too early". Perhaps he has asked her to go to the pub for a drink and take her mind off* her troubles.

My father has put the stereo in his bedroom. He is playing his Jim Reeves* records and staring out of the window. I took him a cup of tea and he said "Thanks, son" in a choked-up* voice.

My mother was looking at old letters in my father's handwriting when I took her tea in; she said, "Adrian, what must you think of us?" I said that Rick Lemon, the youth leader, thinks divorce is society's fault. My mother said, "Bugger society*".

I washed and ironed my school uniform ready for school tomorrow. I am getting quite good at housework.

My spots are so horrific that I can't bear* to write about them. I will be the laughing stock* at school.

I am reading *The Man in the Iron Mask**. I know exactly how he feels.

urgent ['ɜːdʒənt] being important, needing to be done quickly **to take s.o.'s mind off s.th.** to make s.o. forget s.th. **Jim Reeves** singer of sentimental Country-and-Western songs in the 1960s **choked-up** *here: G.* tränenerstickt **bugger society** *sl. contempt.* to hell with society! **to bear** *here: G.* aushalten, ertragen **laughing stock** someone silly whom people laugh at **The Man in the Iron Mask** a novel by Alexandre Dumas about a prisoner in 17th century France who is forced to wear an iron (*G.* eisern) mask all the time

Monday March 16th

Went to school. Found it closed. In my anguish* I had forgotten that I am on holiday. Didn't want to go home, so went to see Bert Baxter instead. He said the social worker had been to see him and had promised to get Sabre a new kennel* but he can't have a home help. (Bert, not Sabre.)

There must have been a full week's washing up in the sink again. Bert says he saves it for me because I make a good job of it. While I washed up I told Bert about my parents getting a divorce. He said he didn't hold with divorce. He said he was married for thirty-five miserable years so why should anybody else get away with it? He told me that he has got four children and that none of them come to see him. Two of them are in Australia so they can't be blamed*, but I think the other two should be ashamed of themselves. Bert showed me a photograph of his dead wife, it was taken in the days before they had plastic surgery*. Bert told me that he was a hostler when he got married (a hostler is somebody doing things with horses) and didn't really notice that his wife looked like a horse until he left to work on the railways. I asked him if he would like to see a horse again. He said he would, so I took him to see Blossom.

It took us ages to get there. Bert walks dead slow and he kept having to sit down on garden walls, but we got there eventually*. Bert said that Blossom was not a horse, she was a girl pony. He kept patting* her and saying "who's a beauty then, eh?" Then Blossom went for a run about so we sat down on the scrap car, and Bert had a Woodbine and I had a Mars bar. Then we walked back to Bert's house. I went to the shops and bought a packet of Vesta* chow mein and a butterscotch Instant Whip* for our dinner, so Bert ate a decent* meal for once. We watched *Pebble Mill at One**, then Bert showed me his old horse brushes and photographs of the big house where he worked when he was a boy. He said he was made into a communist when he was there, but he fell asleep before he could tell me why.

Came home, nobody was in so I played my Abba records at the highest volume until the deaf* woman next door banged* on the wall.

anguish ['æŋgwɪʃ] very great pain **kennel** a small hut for a dog to live in **to blame s.o.** *G.* jemandem Vorwürfe machen **plastic surgery** *G.* plastische Chirurgie **eventually** [ɪ'ventʃʊəlɪ] in the end, finally **to pat** to touch s.o. or s.th. gently with one's hand **butterscotch** a sweet food made from butter and burnt sugar **Vesta/ Instant Whip** trademarks **decent** ['di:snt] proper, pleasant, nice **Pebble Mill At One** a TV programme **deaf** [def] being unable to hear **to bang** to hit loud and hard

Tuesday March 17th

ST PATRICK'S DAY*. BANK HOLIDAY IN N. IRELAND AND REP. OF IRELAND

Looked at *Big and Bouncy*. Measured* my "thing". It was eleven centimetres.

Mr O'Leary who lives across the road from us was drunk at ten o'clock in the morning! He got thrown out of the butcher's for singing.

Wednesday March 18th

My mother and father are both speaking to solicitors*. I expect they are fighting over who gets custody of me. I will be a tug-of-love child*, and my picture will be in the newspapers. I hope my spots clear up before then.

Thursday March 19th

Mr Lucas has put his house up for sale*. My mother says the asking price is thirty thousand pounds!!

What will he do with all that money?

My mother says he will buy another bigger house. How stupid can you get?

If I had thirty thousand pounds I would wander the world having experiences.

I wouldn't take any real money with me because I have read that most foreigners are thieves. Instead I would have three thousand pounds' worth of traveller's cheques sewn* into my trousers. Before I set off*, I would:

a) Send Pandora three dozen red roses.
b) Pay a mercenary* fifty pounds to duff Barry Kent up.
c) Buy the best racing bike in the world and ride it past Nigel's house.
d) Order a massive crate* of expensive dog food so that the dog is properly fed while I'm away.
e) Buy a housekeeper for Bert Baxter.

St Patrick's Day bank holiday in northern Ireland; St Patrick is the patron saint (*G.* Schutzheiliger) of Ireland **to measure** ['meʒə] to find out how long, wide, deep, etc. s.th. is **solicitor** [sə'lɪsɪtə] s.o. who has studied the law and will give people advice in a law case **tug-of-love child** *BE inf.* word used in newspapers when a child's parent tries to get the child back from s.o. else who has been looking after the child **sale** *G.* Verkauf **to sew** [səʊ], **sewed, sewn** *G.* nähen **to set off** to leave **mercenary** ['mɜːsɪnərɪ] a soldier who fights and kills for money **crate** [kreɪt] *G.* Kiste

f) Offer my mother and father a thousand pounds *(each)* to stay together.

When I came back from the world I would be tall, brown and full of ironical experiences and Pandora would cry into her pillow at night because of the chance she missed to be Mrs Pandora Mole. I would qualify to be a vet in record time then I would buy a farmhouse. I would convert* one room into a study so that I could have somewhere quiet to be intellectual in.

I wouldn't waste thirty thousand pounds on buying a semi-detached* house!

Friday March 20th

FIRST DAY OF SPRING. FULL MOON

It is the first day of spring. The council have chopped all the elms* down in Elm Tree Avenue.

Saturday March 21st

My parents are eating different things at different times, so I usually have six meals a day because I don't want to hurt anyone's feelings.

The television is in my room now because they couldn't decide who it belongs to. I can lie in bed and watch the late-night horror.

I am starting to get a bit suspicious* about my mother's feelings towards Mr Lucas. I found a note she had from him; it says: "Pauline how much longer? For God's sake* come away with me. Yours forever, Bimbo."

Although it was signed "Bimbo" I know it was from Mr Lucas because it was written on the back of his red electricity bill*.

My father should be informed. I have put the note under my mattress next to the *Big and Bouncy* magazines.

to convert [kənˈvɜːt] to change **semi-detached house** a house that is joined at one side to another house **elm** *G.* Ulme **suspicious** [səˈspɪʃəs] feeling that s.th. is wrong **for God's sake** (a very inf. expression, used when strongly asking for s. th.) **bill** a list of things which must be paid

Sunday March 22nd

THIRD IN LENT. BRITISH SUMMER TIME BEGINS

It is my grandma's birthday today; she is seventy-six and looks it. I took her a card and a pot plant; it is called Leopard Lily, its foreign name is *Dieffenbachia*. It had a plastic label stuck in the soil which said, "The sap* in this plant is poisonous* so take care". My grandma asked me who chose the plant. I told her my mother did.

My grandma is quite pleased that my parents are getting a divorce! She said that she always thought that my mother had a wanton streak* in her and that now she had been proved right.

I didn't like to hear my mother being spoken of in such a way so I came home. I pretended to grandma that I had promised to meet a friend. But I haven't really got a friend any more, it must be because I'm an intellectual. I expect people are in awe of* me. Looked in my dictionary to find out what "wanton" means. It is not very nice!

Monday March 23rd

Back to school, worse luck! We had Domestic Science today. We did baked potatoes in the oven with cheese filling. My potatoes were bigger than anyone else's so they weren't properly cooked by the time the lesson ended, so I finished them off at Bert Baxter's. He wanted to see Blossom again which was a bit of a drag* because he takes so long to walk anywhere. But we went, anything is better than doing Maths at school.

Bert took his horse brushes with him and gave Blossom a good clean, she was shining like a conker* by the time he'd finished. Bert got out of breath so he sat on the scrap car and had a Woodbine, then we walked back to Bert's house.

Sabre is in a better temper since he got his new kennel and Bert's house is in a better condition as a result of Sabre being outside. Bert told me that the social worker thought he ought to go into an old people's home where he can be properly looked after. Bert doesn't want to. He told a lie to the social worker, he said his grandson came in every day and looked after him. The social worker is going to check up so I could be in trouble for impersonation*!!! I don't know how much more worry I can take*.

sap *G.* Saft **poisonous** *G.* giftig **wanton** ['wɒntən] **streak** *G.* liederlicher, schamloser Charakterzug **to be in awe of** to feel strong respect for **to be a drag** *inf.* to be boring **conker** *G.* Kastanie **impersonation** [ɪmˌpɜːsəˈneɪʃn] pretending to be s.o. else **to take** *here: G.* ertragen, aushalten

Tuesday March 24th

Late last night I saw my mother and Mr Lucas going out in Mr Lucas's car. They went somewhere special because my mother was wearing a boiler suit* with sequins*. She did look a bit wanton. Mr Lucas was wearing his best suit and he had a lot of gold jewellery on. For an old person he certainly knows how to dress.

If my father took more care of his appearance*, none of this would have happened. It stands to reason* that any woman would prefer a man who wears a suit and a lot of gold jewellery to one like my father who hardly ever shaves and wears old clothes and no jewellery.

I am going to stay awake and find out what time my mother comes home.

Midnight. Mother still not home.

2 a.m. No sign of my mother.

Wednesday March 25th
ANNUNCIATION OF B.V. MARY*

Fell asleep, so don't know what time my mother got home. My father said she had gone to the insurance* firm's Christmas dinner and dance. In March! Come off it* dad! I was not born yesterday! We had swimming in Games today. The water was freezing cold and so were the changing cubicles*. I will try to get athlete's foot* so that I don't have to go next week.

Thursday March 26th

Barry Kent has been done by the police for riding a bike without a rear* light. I hope he gets sent to a Detention Centre*. A short sharp shock will do him good.

boiler suit overalls *(AE)* **sequin** ['si:kwɪn] small flat round and shiny piece of metal, sewn onto clothes for decoration **appearance** *here:* what s.o. looks like **to stand to reason** to be clear to sensible people **Annunciation** [əˌnʌnsɪ'eɪʃn] **of B. V. Mary** the day when Mary was told by the angel Gabriel that she was to be the mother of Christ **B. V.** *(short for Latin:* "Beata Virgo") Blessed Virgin **insurance** [ɪn'ʃuərəns] *G.* Versicherung **come off it!** *inf.* stop telling lies! **changing cubicle** very small room for (un)dressing and changing one's clothes **athlete's foot** *G.* Fußpilz **rear** at the back **detention centre** a place where young people who are guilty of a crime are sent to for short periods

Friday March 27th

Pandora and Nigel have split up! It is all round the school. This is the best news I have had for ages.

I am reading *Madame Bovary**, by another frog writer.

Saturday March 28th
LAST QUARTER

Nigel has just left, he is heartbroken. I tried to comfort* him. I said that there are plenty more pebbles* on the beach and fish in the sea. But he was much too upset to listen.

I told him about my suspicions* about my mother and Mr Lucas and he said that it had been going on for a long while. Everybody knew except me and my father!!

We had a long talk about racing bikes, then Nigel went home to think about Pandora.

It is Mother's Day tomorrow. I am in two minds about whether to buy her something or not. I have only got sixty-eight pence.

Sunday March 29th
FOURTH IN LENT. MOTHERING SUNDAY

My father gave me three pounds last night. He said, "Get your mother something decent*, son, it could be the last time". I certainly wasn't going all the way into town for her, so I went to Mr Cherry's and bought a box of Black Magic*, and a card saying "To a wonderful mother".

Card manufacturers* must think that all mothers are wonderful because every single card has "wonderful" written on it somewhere. I felt like crossing* "wonderful" out and putting "wanton" in its place, but I didn't. I signed it "from your son, Adrian". I gave it to her this morning. She said, "Adrian, you shouldn't have". She was right, I shouldn't have.

Must stop now. My mother has arranged what she called "a civilized* meeting". Mr Lucas is going to be there. Naturally *I* am not invited! I am going to listen at the door.

Madame Bovary a famous novel by Gustave Flaubert (1821–1880) about a woman's unhappy marriage and love affair **to comfort** ['kʌmfət] to cheer s.o. up who is sad **pebble** small round stone found in rivers or on the beach **suspicion** [sə'spɪʃn] a feeling that s.th. is wrong **decent** ['di:snt] proper, *here:* nice **Black Magic** (trademark) name for some chocolates **manufacturer** [ˌmænjʊ'fæktʃərə] a person or firm that produces things **to cross out** *G.* durchstreichen **civilized** ['sɪvɪlaɪzd] *here:* pleasant, well-behaved

Monday March 30th

A terrible thing happened last night. My father and Mr Lucas had a fight in the *front* garden, the whole street came outside to watch! My mother tried to separate them but they both told her to "keep out of it". Mr O'Leary tried to help my father, he kept shouting "Give the smarmy* bugger* one for me, George". Mrs O'Leary was shouting horrible things at my mother. By the sound of things she had been watching my mother's movements since Christmas. The civilized meeting broke up at about five o'clock when my father found out how long my mother and Mr Lucas had been in love.

They had another civilized meeting at about seven o'clock, but when my mother disclosed* that she was leaving for Sheffield* with Mr Lucas my father became uncivilized and started fighting. Mr Lucas ran into the garden but my father rugby-tackled* him by the laurel* bush and the fight broke out again. It was quite exciting really. I had a good view from my bedroom window. Mrs O'Leary said, "'Tis* the child I feel sorry for", and all the people looked up and saw me, so I looked especially sad. I expect the experience will give me a trauma* at some stage in the future. I'm all right at the moment, but you never know.

Tuesday March 31st

My mother has gone to Sheffield with Mr Lucas. She had to drive because Mr Lucas couldn't see out of his black eyes. I have informed the school secretary of my mother's desertion*. She was very kind and gave me a form* to give to my father; it is for free school dinners. We are now a single-parent family.

Nigel has asked Barry Kent to stop menacing* me for a few weeks. Barry Kent said he would think about it.

smarmy *BE inf.* unpleasantly and falsely polite **bugger** *BE* taboo (word for a person one does not like) **to disclose** to make known **Sheffield** a large industrial town in the North of England **to rugby-tackle** to stop s.o. by making him/her fall down **laurel** ['lɒrəl] *G.* Lorbeer **'tis** *coll.* it is **trauma** ['trɔːmə] damage to one's mind because of a sudden shock **desertion** [dɪ'zɜːʃn] *here:* running away from s.o. who needs help **form** *G.* Formular **to menace** ['menəs] to threaten (*G.* bedrohen)

Wednesday April 1st

ALL FOOLS' DAY

Nigel rang up this morning and pretended he was an undertaker* and asked when he was to pick up the body. My father answered the phone. Honestly! He has got no sense of humour.

I had a good laugh telling girls that their petticoats* were showing when they weren't. Barry Kent brought a packet of itching powder* into the Art lesson, he put some down Ms Fossington-Gore's flying boots. She is another one without any sense of humour. Barry Kent put some down my back. It wasn't funny. I had to go to the matron* and have it removed*.

The house is looking extremely squalid* because my father is not doing any housework. The dog is pining for* my mother.

I was born exactly thirteen years and three hundred and sixty-four days ago.

Thursday April 2nd

I am fourteen today! Got a track suit and a football from my father. (He is completely insensitive* to my needs.) *A Boy's Book of Carpentry* from my grandma Mole. (No comment.) One pound inside a card from my grandad Sugden. (Last of the big spenders*.) Best of all was ten pounds from my mother and five pounds from Mr Lucas. (Conscience* money.)

Nigel sent a joke card; it said on the front, "Who's sexy, charming intelligent and handsome?". Inside it said, "Well it certainly ain't* you buddy*!!!". Nigel wrote "No offence mate*". He put ten pence inside the envelope.

Bert Baxter sent a card to the school because he doesn't know where I live. His handwriting is dead good, I think it is called "brass plate*". His card had a picture of an alsatian on the front. Inside Bert had written, "Best whishes from Bert and Sabre. P.S. Drain blocked up". Inside the

undertaker s.o. who buries dead people **petticoat** a woman's under-skirt **itching-powder** *G.* Juckpulver **matron** ['meɪtrən] *here:* female nurse in a school **to remove** to take away **squalid** ['skwɒlɪd] dirty, untidy **to pine for s.o.** to miss s.o. very much **insensitive** [ɪn'sensətɪv] not thinking about other people's feelings **big spender** *inf.* s.o. who spends a lot of money **conscience** ['kɒnʃəns] *here: G.* (schlechtes) Gewissen **ain't** *sl.* isn't **buddy** (a word only used by men about men:) friend **mate** *cf.* buddy **brass plate** *G.* Messingschild, -gedenktafel

card there was a book token* for ten shillings. It expired* in December 1958, but it was a kind thought.

So at last I am fourteen! Had a good look at myself in the mirror tonight and I think I can detect* a certain maturity*. (Apart from* the rotten spots.)

Friday April 3rd

Got full marks in the Geography test today. Yes! I am proud to report that I got twenty out of twenty! I was also complimented on the neat presentation of my work. There is nothing I don't know about the Norwegian leather industry. Barry Kent seems to take delight in* being ignorant. When Miss Elf asked him where Norway was in relation* to Britain he said, "First cousin* twice removed*". It hurts me to relate* that even Pandora laughed with the rest of the class. Only Miss Elf and I remained composed*. Unblocked Bert Baxter's drain, it was full of old bones and tea leaves. I told Bert that he really ought to use tea-bags. After all this is the twentieth century! Bert said that he would give them a try. I told him that my mother has run away with an insurance man, he said "Was it an Act of God*?" Then he laughed until his eyes watered.

Saturday April 4th
NEW MOON

Me and my father cleaned the house up today. We had no choice: my grandma is coming for tea tomorrow. We went to Sainsbury's in the afternoon. My father chose a trolley* that was impossible to steer. It also squeaked as if somebody was torturing* mice. I was ashamed to be heard with it. My father chose food that is bad for you. I had to put my foot down* and insist that he bought some fresh fruit and salad. When we got to the check-out* he couldn't find his banker's card, the cashier wouldn't take a cheque without it, so the supervisor had to come and stop the argument. I had to lend my father some of my birthday money. So he

book token *G.* Buchgutschein **to expire** [ɪk'spaɪə] to come to an end **to detect** to discover **maturity** [mə'tjʊərətɪ] *here:* being fully grown-up **apart from** besides, except **to take delight in** to enjoy very much **relation** *G.* 1. Beziehung, 2. Verwandtschaftsverhältnis, Verwandter **first cousin** *G.* Vetter ersten Grades **twice removed** *G.* zweiten Grades **to relate** to tell **composed** calm, self-controlled **Act of God** *G.* "höhere Gewalt" (an expression used in insurance contracts) **trolley** *G.* Einkaufswagen **to torture** ['tɔːtʃə] to cause s.o. great pain **to put one's foot down** *G.* ein Machtwort sprechen **check-out** *G.* Kasse

owes* me eight pounds thirty-eight and a half pence. I made him write an IOU* on the back of the till roll*.

But I must say that I take my hat off to Sainsbury's, they seem to attract a better class of person. I saw a vicar choosing toilet paper; he chose a four-roll pack of purple three-ply*. He must have money to burn*! He could have bought some shiny white and given the difference to the poor. What a hypocrite*!

Sunday April 5th
PASSION SUNDAY*

Nigel came round this morning. He is still mad about Pandora. I tried to take his mind off her by talking about the Norwegian leather industry but he couldn't get interested somehow.

I made my father get up at 1 p.m. I don't see why he should lie stinking in bed all day when I am up and about. He got up and went outside to clean the car. He found one of my mother's earrings down the side of the back seat and he just sat there staring at it. He said, "Adrian, do you miss your mother?" I replied, "Of course I do, but life must go on". He then said, "I don't see why". I took this to mean that he was suicidal*, so I immediately went upstairs and removed* anything harmful from the bathroom.

After we had eaten our frozen roast-beef dinner and I was washing up, he shouted from the bathroom for his razor. I lied and shouted back that I didn't know where it was. I then removed every knife and sharp instrument from the kitchen drawer*. He tried to get his battery razor to work but the batteries had leaked* and gone all green.

I like to think I am broad-minded but the language my father used was beyond the pale*, and all because he couldn't have a shave! Tea was a bit of a drag. My grandma kept saying horrible things about my mother and my father kept rambling on about* how much he missed her. Nobody even noticed I was in the room! The dog got more attention than me!

to owe [əʊ] *G.* schulden **IOU** *short for:* "I owe you" **till roll** *G.* Kassenstreifen **three-ply** ['θri:plaɪ] *G.* dreilagig **to have money to burn** to spend money on unnecessary things **hypocrite** ['hɪpəkrɪt] s.o. who always pretends to be good, friendly, religious, etc. to get some advantage out of it **Passion** ['pæʃn] **Sunday** *G.* Passionssonntag (passion here means the suffering of Christ) **suicidal** [sjʊɪ'saɪdl] wanting to kill oneself **to remove** to take away **drawer** *G.* Schublade **to leak** *G.* auslaufen, undicht sein **beyond the pale** *here:* outside normal social standards **to ramble on about s.th.** to talk about s.th. in a confused way for a long time

My grandma told my father off* for growing a beard. She said, "You may think it amusing to look like a communist, George, but I don't". She said that even in the trenches* at Ypres* my grandad had shaved every day. Sometimes he had to stop rats from eating his shaving soap. She said that my grandad was even shaved by the undertaker when lying in his coffin*, so if the dead could shave there was no excuse for the living. My father tried to explain, but grandma didn't stop talking once so it was a bit difficult.

We were both glad when she went home.

Looked at *Big and Bouncy*. It is Passion* Sunday after all!

Monday April 6th

Had a postcard from my mother. It said "they" were staying with friends until they found a flat. She said I could go and stay for a weekend when they were fixed up*.

I didn't show it to my father.

Tuesday April 7th

My precious* Pandora is going out with Craig Thomas. That's the last time you get a Mars bar from me, Thomas!

Barry Kent is in trouble for drawing a nude* woman in Art. Ms Fossington-Gore said that it wasn't so much the subject matter but his ignorance* of basic biological facts that was so upsetting. I did a good drawing of the Incredible Hulk* smashing Craig Thomas to bits*. Ms Fossington-Gore said it was a "powerful statement of monolithic* oppression*".

Phone call from my mother. Her voice sounded funny as if she had a cold. She kept saying, "You'll understand one day, Adrian". There was a slurping* sound in the background. I expect it was that Lucas creep* kissing her neck. I have seen them do it on the films.

to tell s.o. off *G.* ausschimpfen **trench** *G.* Schützengraben **Ypres** ['iːprə] a Belgian town which was destroyed in many bloody fights during the First World War (1914–1918) **coffin** a box or case in which dead people are buried **passion** ['pæʃn] strong feeling, e.g. of love (but cf. p. 52 **Passion Sunday**!) **to be fixed up** *here:* to settle down **precious** ['preʃəs] beautiful, important **nude** [njuːd] naked **ignorance** knowing nothing **Incredible Hulk** a comic figure of enormous strength **to smash to bits** to break to pieces **monolithic** [ˌmɒnəʊ'lɪθɪk] *fml. here:* huge, very big and strong **oppression** *G.* Unterdrückung **to slurp** *G.* schlürfen **creep** *sl. contempt.* an unpleasant person

Wednesday April 8th

My father wouldn't give me a note excusing me from Games so I spent nearly all morning dressed in pyjamas diving* into a swimming pool and picking up a brick* from the bottom. I had a bath when I came home but I still smell of chlorine. I just don't see the point of the above lesson. When I am grown up I am hardly going to walk along a river bank in my pyjamas am I? And who would be stupid enough to dive into a river for a boring old brick? Bricks are lying around all over the place!

Thursday April 9th

My father and me had a good talk last night. He asked me who I would prefer to live with, him or my mother? I said both. He told me he had made friends with a woman at work, she is called Doreen Slater. He said he would like me to meet her one day. Here we go again; so much for the suicidal, heartbroken, deserted husband!

Friday April 10th

Rang my grandmother to tell her about Doreen Slater. My grandma didn't sound too pleased, she said it was a common-sounding name and I am inclined to* agree with her.

Got *Waiting for Godot** out of the library. Disappointed to find that it was a play. Still, I will give it a go. I have been neglecting* my brain lately.

Nigel asked me if I wanted to stay the weekend. His parents are going to a wedding in Croydon*. My father said I could. He looked quite pleased. I am going round to Nigel's in the morning.

I broke up for the Easter holidays today. Must make sure my brain keeps active.

to dive to swim under water **brick** *G.* Ziegelstein **to be inclined to** to feel a wish to **Waiting for Godot** a play by Samuel Beckett (1952) about two tramps who keep waiting for a mysterious man called Godot (= God?) who never comes **to neglect** to give little attention to **Croydon** a southern district of Greater London

Saturday April 11th

FIRST QUARTER

Nigel is dead lucky. His house is absolutely fantastic! Everything is modern. I don't know what he must think of our house, some of our furniture is over a hundred years old!

His bedroom is massive and he has got a stereo, a *colour* television, a tapedeck, a Scalextric* track*, an electric guitar and amplifier. Spotlights over his bed. Black walls and a white carpet and a racing car continental quilt*. He has got loads of* back issues of *Big and Bouncy*, so we looked through them, then Nigel had a cold shower while I cooked the soup and cut the French loaf. We had a good laugh at *Waiting for Godot*. Nigel had hysterics* when I said that Vladimir* and Estragon* sounded like contraception* pills.

I had a go on Nigel's racing bike. I now want one more than anything in the world. If I had to choose between Pandora and a racing bike, I would choose the bike. Sorry, Pandora, but that's how things are.

We went to the chip shop and had the works*. Fish, chips, pickled onions*, gherkins*, sloppy* peas. Nothing was too expensive for Nigel, he gets loads of pocket money. We walked round for a bit then we came back and watched *The Bug-Eyed* Monster Strikes Back* on the television. I said the bug-eyed monster reminded me of* Mr Scruton the headmaster. Nigel had hysterics again. I think I have got quite a talent to amuse people. I might change my mind about becoming a vet and try writing situation comedy* for television.

When the film finished Nigel said, "How about a nightcap*?" He went to the bar in the corner of the lounge and he poured us both a stiff* whisky and soda. I hadn't actually tasted whisky before and I never will again. How people can drink it for pleasure I don't know. If it was in a medicine bottle they would pour it down the sink!

Don't remember going to bed, but I must have done because I am sitting up in Nigel's parents' bed writing my diary.

Scalextric (trademark) name of a model railway **track** *here:* *G.* Schiene, Spur **continental quilt** *G.* Steppdecke **to have loads of** *inf.* to have a lot of **to have hysterics** [hɪˈsterɪks] *inf. here:* to laugh a lot **Vladimir/Estragon** the two tramps in Beckett's play **contraception** *G.* Verhütung **to have the works** *inf. here:* to have everything **pickled onion** *G.* in Essig eingelegte Zwiebel **gherkin** [ˈgɜːkɪn] *G.* Essiggurke **sloppy** *here:* soft **bug-eyed** having eyes that stick out **to remind s.o. of** to make s.o. think of **situation comedy** TV comedy with scenes from everyday life **nightcap** *here:* alcoholic drink people take before going to bed **stiff** *here:* large and strong

Sunday April 12th
PALM SUNDAY

This weekend with Nigel has really opened my eyes! Without knowing it I have been living in poverty* for the past fourteen years. I have had to put up with inferior* accommodation*, lousy* food and paltry* pocket money. If my father can't provide* a decent standard of living for me on his present salary*, then he will just have to start looking for another job. He is always complaining about having to flog* electric storage heaters anyway. Nigel's father has worked like a slave to create a modern environment* for *his* family. Perhaps if *my* father had built a formica* cocktail bar in the corner of *our* lounge my mother would still be living with us. But oh no. My father actually boasts* about our hundred-year-old furniture.

Yes! Instead of being ashamed of our antiques, he is proud of the clapped-out* old rubbish.

My father should take lessons from Great Literature. Madame Bovary* ran away from that idiot Doctor Bovary because he couldn't supply* her needs.

Monday April 13th

Had a note from Mr Cherry asking me when I can resume* my paper round. I sent a note back to say that due to my mother's desertion I am still in a mental state*. This is true. I wore odd socks* yesterday without knowing it. One was red and one was green. I must pull myself together. I could end up in a lunatic asylum*.

poverty being extremely poor **inferior** [ɪnˈfɪərɪə] worse in quality **accomodation** [əˌkɒməˈdeɪʃn] a place to live in **lousy** *inf. contempt.* very bad **paltry** [ˈpɔːltrɪ] *here:* small **to provide** to give s. o. s. th. that is needed **salary** a monthly pay people get for their work **to flog** *BE inf.* to sell **environment** [ɪnˈvaɪərənmənt] *G.* Umwelt, Umgebung **formica** a strong plastic **to boast** *G.* angeben **clapped-out** *BE inf.* old and no longer working properly **Madame Bovary** the main character in a novel by Flaubert (*cf. p. 48*) **to supply** to give s. o. s. th. that is needed (*cf.* to provide) **to resume** [rɪˈzjuːm] to start again **to be in a mental state** *inf. here:* to be very upset **to wear odd socks** to wear socks of different colour **lunatic asylum** [ˈluːnətɪk əˈsaɪləm] *old use* hospital for people suffering from an illness of the mind

Tuesday April 14th

Had a postcard from my mother. She has found a flat and she wants me to visit her and Lucas as soon as possible.

Why can't my mother write a letter like any normal person? Why should the postman be able to read my confidential* business? Her new address is 79 A, President Carter Walk, Sheffield.

I asked my father if I could go; he said, "Yes, providing she sends the train fare". So I have written a letter asking her to send eleven pounds eighty.

Wednesday April 15th

Went to the youth club with Nigel. It was dead good. We played ping-pong until the balls cracked. Then we had a go on the football table. I beat Nigel fifty goals to thirteen. Nigel went into a sulk* and said that he only lost because his goalkeeper's legs were stuck on with Sellotape* but he was wrong. It was my superior* skill that did it.

A gang of punks passed unkind comments* about my flared trousers* but Rick Lemon, the youth leader, stepped in and led a discussion on personal taste. We all agreed it should be up to the individual to dress how he or she likes. All the same I think I will ask my father if I can have a new pair of trousers. Not many fourteen-year-olds wear flared trousers today, and I don't wish to be conspicuous*.

Barry Kent tried to get in through the fire-doors to avoid paying his five-pence subs*. But Rick Lemon pushed him back outside into the rain. I was very pleased. I owe Barry Kent two pounds' menaces money.

confidential [ˌkɒnfɪˈdenʃl] *here:* private, secret **to go into a sulk** to become bad-tempered and refuse to talk **Sellotape** (trademark) *G.* Klebeband **superior** [suːˈpɪərɪə] *here:* better **to pass comments** to give an opinion, to make remarks **flared trousers** trousers which are very wide towards the lower part of the legs **conspicuous** [kənˈspɪkjʊəs] noticeable, easy to be noticed **subs** *(short for:* subscription) *here: G.* Mitgliedsbeitrag

Thursday April 16th

Got a birthday card from my Auntie Susan, two weeks late! She always forgets the right day. My father said that she's under a lot of pressure because of her job, but I can't see it myself. I'd have thought that being a prison wardress* was dead cushy*, it is only locking and unlocking doors after all. She has sent a present via* the GPO so with luck I should get it by Christmas. Ha! Ha!

Friday April 17th
GOOD FRIDAY*

Poor Jesus, it must have been dead awful for him. I wouldn't have had the guts* to do it myself.

The dog has mauled* the hot-cross buns*; it doesn't respect any traditions.

Saturday April 18th

Got parcel from Auntie Susan. It is an embroidered* toothbrush holder and it was made by one of the prisoners! She is called Grace Pool. Auntie Susan said that I should write and thank her! It is bad enough that my father's sister works in Holloway Prison*. But now I am expected to start writing to the prisoners! Grace Pool could be a murderess or anything!

Still waiting for the eleven pounds eighty pence. It doesn't seem as if my mother is desperate* to see me.

prison wardress a female officer guarding prisoners **cushy** ['kʊʃɪ] *inf.* (of a job:) easy **via** [vaɪə] *Latin* through, by means of **Good Friday** the day when Jesus Christ was nailed to the cross **to have the guts** *inf.* to have the courage **to maul** [mɔːl] *here:* to damage **hot cross bun** *G.* gefülltes Rosinenbrötchen mit einem kleinen Teigkreuz (eaten in Britain on Good Friday) **to embroider** *G.* sticken **Holloway Prison** a large prison in North London **to be desperate** ['despərət] *here:* to want very much

Sunday April 19th
EASTER SUNDAY

Today is the day that Jesus escaped from the cave*. I expect that Houdini* got the idea from him.

My father forgot to go to the bank on Friday so we are penniless. I had to take the pop* bottles back to the shop to buy myself an Easter egg. Watched film, then had a fantastic tea at grandma's. She made a cake covered in little fluffy* chicks*. Some of the fluff got into my father's mouth, he had to have his back thumped* hard. He always manages to spoil things. He has got no Social Decorum* at all. Went to see Bert Baxter after tea. He was pleased to see me and I felt a bit rotten because I have neglected him lately. He gave me a pile* of comics. They are called the *Eagle* and they have got great pictures. I read them until 3 a.m. this morning. Us intellectuals keep anti-social hours. It does us good.

Monday April 20th
BANK HOLIDAY IN UK (EXCEPT SCOTLAND)

My father is in a rage* because the bank is still shut. He has run out of* cigarettes. It will do him good. No sign of the eleven pounds eighty pence.

Wrote to Grace Pool. She is in "D" Wing*. I put:

Dear Miss Pool,

Thank you for making the toothbrush holder. It is charming.

Yours, with kind regards, Adrian

Tuesday April 21st

My father was first in the queue* at the bank this morning. When we got inside the cashier* said he couldn't have any money because he hadn't got any left. My father demanded* to see the manager. I was dead ashamed so I sat behind a plastic plant and waited until the shouting had stopped.

cave a large natural place under the ground **Houdini** (1874–1926) a famous US magician and escapologist (*G.* Entfesselungskünstler) **pop** *inf.* a fizzy drink such as lemonade **fluffy** soft and feathery **chick** a baby bird, esp. a chicken **to thump** to hit hard **social decorum** [dɪ'kɔːrəm] right and proper behaviour **pile** a group of things lying one upon another **rage** a great anger **to run out of s.th.** to have nothing left of s.th. **wing** *here:* a part of a large building **queue** a line of people waiting for s.th. **cashier** [kæ'ʃɪə] s.o. who works in a bank **to demand** to ask strongly

Mr Niggard*, the head* bloke*, came out and calmed my father down. He said he would arrange a temporary* overdraft*. My father looked dead pathetic*, he kept saying, "It was that bloody* vet's bill". Mr Niggard looked as if he understood. Perhaps he has got a mad dog as well. We can't be the only ones, can we?

The eleven pounds, etc., came by second post* so I am going to Sheffield tomorrow morning. I've never been on a train on my own before. I am certainly stretching my wings lately.

Wednesday April 22nd

My father gave me a lift to the station. He also gave me a bit of advice about the journey; he said I was not to buy a pork pie* from the buffet car*.

I stood in the train with my head out of the window and my father stood on the platform. He kept looking at his watch. I couldn't think of anything to say and neither could he. In the end I said, "Don't forget to feed the dog, will you?" My father gave a nasty laugh, then the train started to move so I waved and went to look for a non-smoking seat. All the filthy* smokers were crammed together* choking and coughing. They were a rough-looking, noisy lot* so I hurried through their small carriage holding my breath. The non-smoking carriages seemed to have a quieter type of person in them. I found a window seat opposite an old lady. I had wanted to look at the landscape or read my book but the old bat* started on about her daughter's hysterectomy* and telling me things I didn't want to hear. She just about sent me barmy*! It was nag*, nag, nag. But thank God she got off at Chesterfield*. She left her *Woman's Own** behind so I had a good laugh at the Problem Page, read the story, and then the train slowed down for Sheffield. My mother started crying when she saw me. It was a bit embarrassing but quite nice at the same

niggard *contempt.* s.o. who is unwilling to spend money **head** *here:* s.o. who is in charge **bloke** *BE inf.* a man **temporary** ['tempərərɪ] only for a short time **overdraft** *G.* Kontoüberziehung **pathetic** *here contempt.* helpless, weak **bloody** *BE very inf.* (a word showing anger) **second post** second-class postage is a cheaper way of sending letters which then take a bit longer than those sent by first-class **pork pie** *G.* Schweinepastete **buffet** ['bʊfeɪ] **car** the part of a train where people can buy sandwiches, tea, etc. **filthy** very dirty **to be crammed together** to be sitting very close together **a lot** *here inf.* a crowd **bat** *here inf.* s.o. who is a bit mad **hysterectomy** [ˌhɪstə'rektəmɪ] *G.* operative Entfernung der Gebärmutter **barmy** *inf.* mad **to nag** to complain to s.o. without end **Chesterfield** a town in North central England **Woman's Own** a popular illustrated weekly magazine for women

time. We got a taxi from the station, Sheffield looks OK, just like home really. I didn't see any knife and fork factories. I expect Margaret Thatcher* has closed them all down.

Lucas was out flogging* insurance so I had my mother all to myself until eight o'clock. The flat is dead grotty*, it is modern but small. You can hear the neighbours coughing. My mother is used to better things. I am dead tired, so will stop.

I hope my father is being kind to the dog. I wish my mother would come home, I had forgotten how nice she is.

Thursday April 23rd
ST GEORGE'S DAY*

Me and mum went shopping today. We bought a Habitat* lampshade for her bedroom and a new pair of trousers for me. They are dead good, really tight.

We had a Chinese Businessman's Lunch and then went to see a Monty Python film* all about the life of Jesus. It was dead daring*, I felt guilty laughing.

Lucas was at the flat when we got back. He had got the dinner ready but I said I wasn't hungry and I went to my room. It would choke me to eat anything that creep had touched! Later on I phoned my father from a call-box; I just had time to shout, "Don't forget to feed the dog", before the pips went.

Retired* to bed early because of all the slopping* Lucas was doing. He calls my mother "Paulie" when he knows very well that her name is Pauline.

Margaret Thatcher Conservative British Prime Minister (1979–1990) **to flog** *BE inf.* to sell **grotty** *inf.* unpleasant **St George** the patron saint (*G.* Schutzheiliger) of England **Habitat** (trademark) the name of a firm selling furniture **Monty Python** ['paɪθn] a famous group of British comedians, one of whose films is *The Life Of Brian*, a nonsense version of the life of Jesus **daring** ['deərɪŋ] very brave **to retire** *here:* to go away to rest **to slop** *inf. here: G.* rührseliges Zeug reden

Friday April 24th

Helped my mother to paint her kitchen. She is doing it brown and cream, it looks awful, just like the toilets at school. Lucas bought me a penknife*. He is trying to bribe* me into liking him again. Hard luck, Lucas! Us Moles never forget. We are just like the Mafia, once you cross* us we bear a grudge* all our lives. He has stolen a wife and mother so he will have to pay the price! It is a shame because the penknife is full of gadgets* that would be useful to me in my everyday life.

Saturday April 25th

Lucas doesn't work on Saturdays so I had to put up with* his lechery* all day. He is constantly touching my mother's hand or kissing her or putting his arm round her shoulders, I don't know how she stands it, it would drive me mad.

Lucas drove us out into the countryside this afternoon, it was hilly and high up. I got cold so I sat in the car and watched my mother and Lucas making an exhibition of themselves*. Thank God, no members of the public were around. It is not a pretty sight to see old people running up hills laughing.

Came back, had a bath, thought about the dog, went to sleep.

Home tomorrow.

3 a.m. Just had a dream about stabbing* Lucas with the toothpick* on my penknife. Best dream I've had for ages.

Sunday April 26th

2.10 p.m. So my little sojourn* in Sheffield is drawing to a close*. I am catching the 7.10 p.m. train, which only leaves five hours to do my packing. My father was right. I didn't need two suitcases of clothes. Still it is better to be safe than sorry*, I always say. I shan't be sorry to leave this sordid* flat with the coughing neighbours, though naturally I have some

penknife small knife that can be closed and put into one's pocket **to bribe** *G.* bestechen **to cross s.o.** to make s.o. angry **to bear a grudge** to have unfriendly feelings towards s.o. **gadget** ['gædʒɪt] *G.* Vorrichtung **to put up with** to accept, to tolerate **lechery** ['letʃərɪ] *G.* Lüsternheit **to make an exhibition of oneself** to behave stupidly in public **to stab** to wound or kill with a knife, etc. **toothpick** *G.* Zahnstocher **sojourn** ['sɒdʒɜːn] *fml.* a short stay **to draw to a close** to come to an end **better to be safe than sorry!** *proverb* it's better to avoid risks **sordid** dirty, unpleasant

regrets about my mother's stubbornness* in refusing to come home with me.

I told her that the dog was pining to death for her but she rang my father up and like a fool he told her that the dog had just eaten a whole tin of Pedigree Chum* and a bowl of Winalot*.

I told her about my father and Doreen Slater, hoping to send her mad with jealousy*, but she just laughed and said, "Oh is Doreen still making the rounds?" I have done my best to get her back, but must admit* defeat*.

11 p.m. Journey back a nightmare*, non-smoking compartments all full, forced to share carriage with pipes, cigars and cigarettes. Queued for twenty minutes for a cup of coffee in the buffet. Just got to the counter when the grille* came down and the man put up a sign saying: "Closed due to signal failure*!" Got back to seat, found a soldier in my place. Found another seat, but had to endure* maniac* sitting opposite telling me he had a radio inside his head controlled by Fidel Castro*.

My father met me at the station, the dog jumped up to meet me, missed, and nearly fell in front of the 9.23 p.m. Birmingham* express.

My father said he had had Doreen Slater for tea. By the state of the house I should think he'd had her for breakfast, dinner and tea! I have never seen the woman, but from the evidence* she left behind I know she has got bright red hair, wears orange lipstick and sleeps on the left side of the bed.

What a homecoming!

My father said Doreen had ironed my school clothes ready for the morning. What did he expect? Thanks?

stubborness ['stʌbənnɪs] being unwilling to change one's mind **Pedigree Chum/ Winalot** (trademark) names of dog food **jealousy** ['dʒeləsɪ] *G.* Eifersucht **to admit** to agree that s.th. is true **defeat** having lost a fight **nightmare** ['naɪtmeə] a terrible and frightening dream **grille** *G.* Fenstergitter **failure** opposite of success **to endure** [ɪn'djʊə] to suffer s.th. calmly **maniac** ['meɪnɪæk] a dangerously mad person **Fidel Castro** Communist leader of Cuba since 1959 **Birmingham** Britain's second largest city (about 900,000 people) **evidence** *G.* Beweis

Monday April 27th

Mrs Bull taught us to wash up in Domestic Science. Talk about teaching your grandmother to suck eggs*! I must be one of the best washer-uppers in the world! Barry Kent broke an unbreakable plate so Mrs Bull sent him out of the room. I saw him smoking quite openly in the corridor. He has certainly got a nerve! I felt it was my duty to report him to Mrs Bull. I did this purely out of concern* for Barry Kent's health. He was taken to pop-eye Scruton and his Benson and Hedges* were confiscated. Nigel said he saw Mr Scruton smoking them in the staff room at dinner-time, but surely this can't be true?

Pandora and Craig Thomas are creating a scandal by flaunting* their sexuality in the playground. Miss Elf had to knock on the staff-room window and ask them to stop kissing.

Tuesday April 28th

Mr Scruton made a speech in assembly this morning. It was about the country's lack of morals, but really he was talking about Pandora and Craig Thomas. The speech didn't do any good because while we were singing "There is a Green Hill Far Away", I distinctly saw glances* of a passionate* nature pass between them.

Wednesday April 29th

My father is worried, electric storage heaters are not selling well. My father says this proves that consumers are not as stupid as everyone thinks. I'm fed up with him mooning about* the house at night. I have advised him to join a club or get a hobby but he is determined* to feel sorry for himself. The only time he laughs is when those advertisements for electric storage heaters are shown on televison. Then he laughs himself silly.

to teach your grandmother to suck eggs *inf. proverb* to try and teach people s.th. they can already do very well **concern** [kən'sɜːn] *here:* worry **Benson and Hedges** (trademark) a name for cigarettes **to flaunt** [flɔːnt] to show openly **glance** a quick look **passionate** showing strong feeling **to moon about** to spend a lot of time doing nothing because one is unhappy **determined** [dɪ'tɜːmɪnd] having made up one's mind, being decided

Thursday April 30th

I was seriously menaced at school today. Barry Kent threw my snaplock executive* brief-case* on to the rugby pitch*. I have got to find two pounds quickly before he starts throwing *me* on to the rugby pitch. It's no good asking my father for money, he is in despair* because of all the red bills*.

Friday May 1st

Grandma rang early this morning to say "Cast ne'er a clout till May be out*". I haven't got the faintest idea* what she was going on about. All I know is that it has something to do with vests.

I am pleased to report that Barry Kent and his gang have been banned from the Off The Streets youth club. (But this means that they are now *on* the streets, worse luck.) They filled a French letter* with water and threw it at a bunch* of girls and made them scream. Pandora burst the thing with a badge* pin and Rick Lemon came out of his office and slipped in the water. Rick was dead mad, he got dirty marks all over his yellow trousers. Pandora helped Rick to throw the gang out, she looked dead fierce*. I expect she will win the medal for "Most helpful member of the year".

Saturday May 2nd

Had a letter from Grace Pool! This is what it said:

> Dear Adrian,
>
> Thank you for your charming letter of thanks. It fair* brightened up my day. The girls are all joshing me about* my suitor*. I am due for parole* on June 15th, would it be possible to come and see you?

executive [ɪg'zekjʊtɪv] *here inf.* expensive **brief-case** ['bri:fkeɪs] *G.* Aktentasche **pitch** *here:* field **to be in despair** to have no hope **red bill** *G.* Mahnschreiben **cast ne'er a clout till May be out** *arch. proverb* don't throw (cast) your warm clothes ("clout") away before the end of May! **not to have the faintest idea** not to understand at all **French letter** *sl.* condom **bunch** *inf.* a group **badge** *G.* Plakette, Button **fierce** [fɪəs] wild **fair** here used instead of fairly: completely, quite **to josh s.o.** *AE inf.* to make fun of s.o. **suitor** *old use* a man who wants to marry a woman **parole** [pə'rəʊl] letting people out of prison after they have promised to behave well in future **to be due for** *G.* an der Reihe sein mit

Your Auntie Susan is one of the best screws* in here, that's why I obliged* and made the toothbrush holder. See you on the fifteenth then.

Yours with fond* regards*,

Grace Pool

P.S. I was falsely convicted* of arson* but that is all in the past now. My God! What shall I do?

Sunday May 3rd
SECOND AFTER EASTER

There is nothing left in the freezer, nothing in the pantry* and only slimming bread* in the bread bin. I don't know what my father does with all the money. I was forced to go round to grandma's before I died from malnutrition*. At four o'clock I had one of those rare moments of happiness that I will remember all my life. I was sitting in front of grandma's electric coal fire eating dripping toast and reading the *News of the World**. There was a good play on Radio Four* about torturing* in concentration camps. Grandma was asleep and the dog was being quiet. All at once I felt this dead good feeling. Perhaps I am turning religious.

I think I have got it in me to be a Saint* of some kind.

Phoned Auntie Susan but she is on duty in Holloway. Left a message with her friend Gloria, asking Auntie Susan to ring me urgently.

Monday May 4th
BANK HOLIDAY IN UK. NEW MOON

Auntie Susan rang to say that Grace Pool has had her parole cancelled* because she set fire to the embroidery* workshop and destroyed a gross* of toothbrush holders.

Their loss is my gain*!

screw *sl.* a prison officer **to oblige (s.o.)** *here:* to do s.th. nice for s.o. **fond** *here:* loving **regards** *here:* wishes, greetings **to be convicted of** to be sent to prison because of **arson** ['ɑːsn] setting fire to a house or other building **pantry** ['pæntrɪ] a small room where the food is kept **slimming bread** diet bread **malnutrition** [ˌmælnjuːˈtrɪʃn] *fml.* eating unhealthy food **News of the World** a popular Sunday newspaper with articles about scandals and sex crimes **Radio Four** a BBC channel with educational programmes, discussions, etc. **to torture** ['tɔːtʃə] to make s.o. suffer very much **saint** *G.* Heilige(r) **to cancel** to stop from happening, to call off **embroidery** *G.* Stickerei **gross** [grəʊs] a group of 144 things **gain** profit, advantage

Tuesday May 5th

Saw our postman on the way to school, he said that my mother is coming to visit me on Saturday. I've a good mind to* report him to the Postmaster General* for reading a person's private postcard!

My father had also read my postcard by the time I got home from school. He looked pleased and started cleaning rubbish out of the lounge, then he rang Doreen Slater and said he would have to "take a rain check on* Saturday's flick*". Grown ups are always telling adolescents to speak clearly then they go and talk a lot of gibberish* themselves. Doreen Slater shouted down the phone. My father shouted back that he "didn't want a long-term relationship", he had "made that clear from the start", and that "nobody could replace* his Pauline". Doreen Slater went shrieking* on and on until my father slammed the phone down. The phone kept ringing until my father took the phone off the hook. He went mad doing housework until 2 a.m. this morning, and it's only Tuesday! What will he be like on Saturday morning? The poor fool is convinced* that my mother is coming back for good*.

Wednesday May 6th

I am proud to report that I have been made a school-dinner monitor*. My duties are to stand at the side of the pig bin* and make sure that my fellow pupils scrape* their plates properly.

Thursday May 7th

Bert Baxter rang the school to ask me to call round urgently. Mr Scruton told me off, he said the school telephone was not for the convenience* of the pupils. Get stuffed*, Scruton, you pop-eyed git!!! Bert was in a terrible state. He had lost his false teeth. He has had them since 1946, they have got sentimental value* for him because they used to belong to his father. I looked everywhere for them, but couldn't find them.

to have a good mind to to want to **Postmaster General** the highest official of the national Post Service **to take a rain check on s.th.** *AE* not to want to accept s.th. straight away **flick** *inf.* film **gibberish** ['dʒɪbərɪʃ] *contempt.* nonsense **to replace** to take the place of **to shriek** [ʃriːk] to shout in a loud and high voice **to be convinced** to be sure **for good** for ever **monitor** *here:* a pupil who is chosen to do special duties **bin** *G.* Abfallbehälter, Tonne **to scrape** *here: G.* sauber kratzen **convenience** [kən'viːnjəns] *here:* use **get stuffed** sl. (expression showing great anger) **value** *G.* Wert

I went to the shops and bought him a tin of soup and a butterscotch* Instant Whip. It was all he could manage at the moment. I have promised to go round tomorrow and look again. Sabre was happy for once; he was chewing something in his kennel.

My father is still cleaning the house up. Even Nigel commented on how clean the kitchen floor looked. I wish my father wouldn't wear the apron though, he looks like a poofter* in it.

Friday May 8th

Found Bert's teeth in Sabre's kennel. Bert rinsed* them under the tap and put them back in his mouth! This is the most revolting* thing I have ever seen.

My father has got bunches of flowers to welcome my mother home. They are all over the house stinking the place out.

Mr Lucas's house has been sold at last. I saw the estate agent's* minion* putting the board up. I hope the new people are respectable. I am reading the *Mill on the Floss**, by a bloke* called George Eliot*.

Saturday May 9th

I was woken up at 8.30 by a loud banging on the front door. It was an Electricity Board* official. I was amazed to hear that he had come to turn off our electricity! My father owes £ 95.79 p. I told the official that we needed electricity for life's essentials* like the television and stereo, but he said that people like us are sapping* the country's strength. He went to the meter cupboard*, did something with tools, and the second hand on the kitchen clock stopped. It was dead symbolic. My father came in from fetching the *Daily Express*. He was whistling and looking dead cheerful. He even asked the official if he would like a cup of tea! The official said, "No thank you", and hurried up the path and got into his little blue van. My father switched the electric kettle on. I was forced to tell him.

butterscotch *cf. p. 43* **poofter** *sl.* male homosexual **to rinse** to wash quickly **revolting** unpleasant, disgusting **estate agent** *BE* s.o. whose job it is to sell houses **minion** *fml.* ['mɪnjən] s.o. who has to carry out s.o. else's orders **The Mill on the Floss**, a novel by **George Eliot** (1819–1880), a woman (!) whose real name was Mary Anne Evans **bloke** *inf.* man **electricity board** *G.* Elektrizitätsgesellschaft **essentials** [ɪ'senʃlz] things people cannot live without **to sap** to destroy s.th. slowly **meter cupboard** *G.* Stromzählerkasten

Naturally I got the blame! My father said I should have refused entry*. I told him that he should have put all the bill money away each week like grandma does. But he just went berserk*. My mother turned up with Lucas! It was just like old times with everybody shouting at once. I took the dog to the shops and bought five boxes of candles. Mr Lucas lent me the money.

When I got back I stood in the hall and heard my mother say, "No wonder you can't pay the bills, George; just look at all these flowers. They must have cost a fortune*". She said it very kindly. Mr Lucas said he would lend my father a "ton*" but my father was very dignified* and said, "All I want from you, Lucas, is my wife". My mother complimented my father on how nicely he was keeping the house. My father just looked sad and old. I felt dead sorry for him.

I was sent outside while they talked about who was getting custody of me, the arguing went on for ages. In fact until it was time to light the candles.

Lucas spilt* candle-wax over his new suede* shoes. It was the only cheerful incident in a tragic day.

When my mother and Lucas had gone off in a taxi I went to bed with the dog. I heard my father talking to Doreen Slater on the phone, then the front door slammed and I looked out of my window to see him driving off in the car. The back seat was full of flowers.

Sunday May 10th

THIRD AFTER EASTER. MOTHER'S DAY. USA AND CANADA. MOON'S FIRST QUARTER

Didn't get up until half-past four this afternoon. I think I am suffering from depression. Nothing happened at all today, apart from a hail* storm around six o'clock.

entry coming in, entering **to go beserk** to become very violent **to cost a fortune** to be very expensive **ton** *sl.* £ 100 **dignified** ['dɪgnɪfaɪd] impressive **to spill, spilt, spilt** to pour out without wanting to **suede** [sweɪd] soft fine leather **hail** frozen drops of rain

Monday May 11th

Bert Baxter offered to lend us a paraffin heater. Our gas central heating won't work without electricity. I thanked him but refused his kind offer. I have read that they are easily knocked over and our dog would no doubt cause a towering* inferno*.

If it gets out* that our electricity has been cut off, I will cut my throat*. The shame would be too much to bear.

Tuesday May 12th

Had a long talk with Mr Vann the Careers teacher* today. He said that if I want to be a vet I will have to do Physics, Chemistry and Biology for O level*. He said that Art, Woodwork and Domestic Science won't do much good.

I am at the Crossroads* in my life. The wrong decision now could result in a tragic loss to the veterinary world. I am hopeless at science. I asked Mr Vann which O levels you need to write situation comedy for televison. Mr Vann said that you don't need qualifications at all, you just need to be a moron*.

Wednesday May 13th

Had an in-depth* talk about O levels with my father, he advised me to only do the subjects that I am good at. He said that vets spend half their working life with their hands up cows' bums*, and the other half injecting* spoiled fat dogs. So I am rethinking my future career prospects.

I wouldn't mind being a sponge-diver*, but I don't think there is much call* for them in England.

towering frightening and gigantic **inferno** *here:* a huge fire **to get out** *here:* to become known **throat** the front part of the neck **Careers teacher** a teacher who gives pupils advice about exams, jobs, etc. **O level** school-leaving exam, taken in one or more subjects at the age of 15 or 16 *(cf. p. 32 GCE)* **crossroads** a place where two roads meet **moron** ['mɔːrɒn] *BE inf. contempt.* fool, idiot **in-depth** *here:* full of details, thorough **bum** *BE inf.* the part of the body that one sits on **to inject** to put medicine into s.o. with the help of a needle **sponge-diver** *G.* Seeschwammtaucher **call** *here:* need, demand

Thursday May 14th

Miss Sproxton told me off because my English essay was covered in drops of candle-wax. I explained that I had caught my overcoat sleeve on the candle whilst doing my homework. Her eyes filled with tears and she said I was "a dear brave lad", and she gave me a merit mark*.

After supper of cream crackers* and tuna fish, played cards in the candlelight. It was dead good. My father cut the ends off our gloves, we looked like two criminals on the run.

I am reading *Hard Times**, by Charles Dickens*.

Friday May 15th

My grandmother has just made a surprise visit. She caught us huddled* round our new Camping-gaz stove* eating cold beans out of a tin. My father was reading *Playboy* under cover of* the candlelight and I was reading *Hard Times* by my key-ring torch*. We were quite contented*. My father had just said that it was a "good training for when civilization collapses" when grandma burst in and started having hysterics. She has forced us to go to her house so I am there now sleeping in my dead grandad's bed. My father is sleeping downstairs on two armchairs pushed together. Grandma has written a Giro cheque for the electricity money, she is furious because she wanted the money for restocking* her freezer. She buys two dead cows a year.

Saturday May 16th

Helped grandma with the weekend shopping. She was dead fierce in the grocer's; she watched the scales* like a hawk watching a fieldmouse. Then she pounced* and accused the shop assistant of giving her underweight bacon. The shop assistant was dead scared of* her and put another slice* on.

merit mark *here: G.* Pluspunkt **cream cracker** a biscuit eaten with butter and cheese **Hard Times** a novel by **Charles Dickens** (1812–1870) about the hard life of working class people in an industrial town in the north of England **to huddle** to be together in a very small group **stove** *G.* Herd **under cover of** hidden by **torch** *G.* (Taschen-) Lampe **contented** happy with what one has got **to restock** to fill s.th. up again **scales** *G.* Waage **to pounce** to notice s.th. at once and make a sharp remark about it **to be scared** [skeəd] to be frightened **slice** a thin flat piece cut from s.th.

Our arms were dead tired by the time we'd staggered* up the hill carrying big bags of shopping. I don't know how my grandma does it when she's alone. I think the council ought to put escalators on hills; they would save money in the long run*, old people wouldn't go about collapsing all over the place. My father paid the electricity bill at the post office today, but it will be at least a week before the computer gives permission* for our electricity to be reconnected*.

Sunday May 17th

My grandma made us get up early and go to church with her. My father was made to comb his hair and wear one of his dead father's ties. Grandma held both our arms and looked proud to be with us. The church service was dead boring. The vicar looked like the oldest man alive and spoke in a feeble* sort of voice. My father kept standing up when we were supposed to sit down and vice versa. I copied what grandma did, she is always right. My father sang too loudly, everyone looked at him. I shook the vicar's hand when we were allowed outside. It was like touching dead leaves.

After dinner we listened to my grandma's records of Al Jolson, then grandma went upstairs for a sleep and my father and me washed up. My father broke a forty-one-year-old milk jug*! He had to go out for a drink to recover* from the shock. I went to see Bert Baxter but he wasn't in, so I went to see Blossom instead. She was very pleased to see me. It must be dead boring standing in a field all day long. No wonder she welcomes visitors.

Monday May 18th

Grandma is not speaking to my father because of the milk jug. Can't wait to get home where things like milk jugs don't matter.

to stagger to walk very unsteadily **in the long run** in the end **permission** agreement **to reconnect** *here: G.* wieder anschließen **feeble** weak **jug** *BE* a pot with a handle, used for water, milk beer, etc. **to recover** to get well again after being ill or shocked

Tuesday May 19th
FULL MOON

My father is in trouble for staying out late last night. Honestly! He is the same age as the milk jug so surely he can come in what time he likes!

Told my father about being menaced today. I was forced to because Barry Kent seriously damaged my school blazer and tore the school badge* off. My father is going to speak to Barry Kent tomorrow *and* he is going to get all the menaces money back off him, so it looks like I could be rich!

Wednesday May 20th

Barry Kent denied* all knowledge of menacing me and laughed when my father asked him to repay the money. My father went to see his father and had a serious argument and threatened* to call the police. I think my father is dead brave. Barry Kent's father looks like a big ape and has got more hair on the back of his hands than my father has got on his entire* head.

The police have said that they can't do anything without proof* so I am going to ask Nigel to give them a sworn statement* that he has seen me handing menaces money over.

Thursday May 21st

Barry Kent duffed me up in the cloakroom today. He hung me on one of the coathooks*. He called me a "coppers' nark*" and other things too bad to write down. My grandma found out about the menacing (my father didn't want her to know on account of* her diabetes). She listened to it all then she put her hat on, thinned her lips and went out. She was gone one hour and seven minutes, she came in, took her coat off, fluffed* her hair out, took £ 27.18 from the anti-mugger belt* round her waist*. She said, "He won't bother* you again, Adrian, but if he does, let me know". Then she got the tea ready. Pilchards*, tomatoes and ginger

school badge *G.* Schulabzeichen, -wappen **to deny** [dɪ'naɪ] to say that s. th. is not true **to threaten** ['θretn] *G.* (be)drohen **entire** [ɪn'taɪə] whole **proof** information that shows that s. th. is true **sworn statement** *G.* eidesstattliche Erklärung **coathook** *here:* a piece of metal for hanging clothes on **copper's nark** *sl.* s. o. who gives information to the police **on account of** because of **to fluff out** *here:* to shake **anti-mugger belt** a belt in which money can be hidden so that robbers (*inf.* muggers) cannot steal it **waist** *G.* Taille **to bother** to trouble s. o. **pilchard** ['pɪltʃəd] *G.* Sardine

cake*. I bought her a box of diabetic chocolates from the chemist's as a token of my esteem*.

Friday May 22nd

It is all round the school that an old lady of seventy-six frightened Barry Kent and his dad into returning* my menaces money. Barry Kent daren't* show his face. His gang are electing* a new leader.

Saturday May 23rd

Home again, the electricity has been reconnected. All the plants are dead. Red bills on the doormat.

Sunday May 24th
ROGATION SUNDAY*

I have decided to paint my room black; it is a colour I like. I can't live a moment longer with Noddy* wallpaper. At my age it is positively indecent to wake up to Big Ears* and all the rest of the Toyland* idiots running around the walls. My father says I can use any colour I like so long as I buy the paint and do it myself.

Monday May 25th

I have decided to be a poet. My father said that there isn't a suitable career structure* for poets and no pensions and other boring things, but I am quite decided. He tried to interest me in becoming a computer operator, but I said, "I need to put my soul into my work and it is well known that computers haven't got a soul". My father said, "The Americans are working on it". But I can't wait that long.

Bought two tins of black vinyl silk*-finish* paint and a half-inch* brush. Started painting as soon as I got home from the DIY* centre. Noddy keeps showing through the black paint. Looks like it'll need two coats*. Just my luck!

ginger cake *G.* Lebkuchen **token of esteem** a sign of respect **to return** *here:* to give back **to dare to do s.th.** to be brave enough to do s.th. **to elect** [ɪ'lekt] to choose s.o. for an office **Rogation Days** special days in the Church of England for prayers asking for a good harvest (harvest *G.* Ernte) **Noddy** a popular character from a children's book by Enid Blyton (1951), living with his friend **Mr Big Ears** in **Toyland** **career structure** *here: G.* (gesicherte) Laufbahn **silk** *G.* Seide **finish** *here: G.* Deckanstrich. **inch** 2.54 cm **DIY** *short for:* do-it-yourself **coat** *here: G.* Anstrich, Schicht

Tuesday May 26th
MOON'S LAST QUARTER

Now put on two coats of black paint! Noddy still showing through! Black paw-marks over landing and stairs. Can't get paint off hands. Hairs falling out of brush. Fed up with whole thing. Room looks dark and gloomy. Father hasn't lifted a finger to help. Black paint everywhere.

Wednesday May 27th

Third coat. Slight improvement, only Noddy's hat showing through now.

Thursday May 28th
ASCENSION DAY*

Went over Noddy's hat with kid's paintbrush and last of black paint, but bloody hat bells are still showing through!

Friday May 29th

Went over hat bells with black felt-tip pen, did sixty-nine tonight, only a hundred and twenty-four to go.

Saturday May 30th

Finished last bell at 11.25 p.m. Know just how Rembrandt* must have felt after painting the Sistine Chapel* in Venice.

2 a.m. The paint is dry but it must have been faulty because it is all streaky*, and here and there you can see Gollywog's* striped trousers and Mr Plod's* nose. Thank God the bloody bells don't show through! My father has just been in to tell me to go to sleep, he said my room reminded him of a Salvador Dali* painting. He said it was a surrealist* nightmare, but he is only jealous because he has got yukky roses on his bedroom walls.

Ascension [əˈsenʃn] **Day** a Christian festival day, held on the 40th day after Easter (*G.* Christi Himmelfahrt) **Rembrandt** (1606–1669)/**Salvador Dali** (1904–1989) famous painters **Sistine** [ˈsɪstiːn] **Chapel** *G.* Sixtinische Kapelle (this chapel is in Rome (!) and its roof was painted by Michelangelo, not by Rembrandt) **streaky** having stripes **Gollywog/Mr Plod** fellow-characters of Noddy **surrealist** [səˈrɪəlɪst] *here:* strange, fantastic, bizarre

Sunday May 31st

SUNDAY AFTER ASCENSION

I bought a joss stick* from Mr Singh's shop. I lit it in my room to try and get rid of the paint smell. My father came into my room and threw the joss stick out of the window, he said he "wouldn't have me messing with* drugs"! I tried to explain but my father was too angry to listen. I stayed in my room for a few hours but the black walls seemed to be closing in on me so I went to see Bert Baxter. Couldn't make him hear, so I came home and watched religion on the televison. Had tea, did Geography homework, went to bed. Dog won't stay in room any more; it whimpers* to be let out.

Monday June 1st

BANK HOLIDAY IN THE REP. OF IRELAND

My father had a letter that made his face go white: he has been made redundant* from his job! He will be on the dole*! How can we live on the pittance* that the government will give us? The dog will have to go! It costs thirty-five pence a day for dog food, not counting Winalot. I am now a single-parent child whose father is on the dole! Social Security* will be buying my shoes!

I didn't go to school today, I rang the school secretary and told her that my father is mentally ill and needs looking after. She sounded dead worried and asked if he was violent. I said that he hadn't shown any signs of being violent, but if he started I would call the doctor. I made my father lots of hot, sweet drinks for shock, he kept going on about electric storage heaters and saying that he would spill the beans* to the media*.

He rang Doreen Slater up and she came round straightaway, she had a horrible little kid called Maxwell with her. It was quite a shock to see Doreen Slater for the first time. Why my father wanted to have carnal knowledge* of her I can't imagine. She is as thin as a stick insect*. She has got no bust and no bum.

joss stick *G.* Räucherstäbchen **to mess with** *AE inf.* to play about with s.th. dangerous **to whimper** to make low unhappy sounds **to be made redundant** to become unemployed **to be on the dole** to get unemployment money **pittance** *contempt.* a very small sum of money **Social Security** *G.* Sozialhilfe **to spill the beans** *inf.* to tell s.o. a secret **(mass) media** *(Latin plural)* TV, newspapers, radio **to have carnal knowledge of s.o.** *very fml.* to have sexual intercourse with s.o. **stick insect** an insect with a long thin body and legs

She is just straight all the way up and down, including her nose and mouth and hair. She put her arms round my father as soon as she came into the house. Maxwell started to cry, the dog started to bark, so I went back to my black room and counted how many things were now showing through the paint: a hundred and seventeen!

Doreen left at 1.30 p.m. to take Maxwell to play-school*. She did some shopping for us then cooked a sloppy sort of meal made of spaghetti and cheese. She is a one-parent family; Maxwell was born out of wedlock*. She told me about herself when we were washing up. She would be quite nice if she were a bit fatter.

Tuesday June 2nd

NEW MOON

Doreen and Maxwell stayed the night. Maxwell was supposed to sleep on the sofa, but he cried so much that he ended up sleeping in the double bed between my father and Doreen, so my father was unable to extend* his carnal knowledge of Doreen. He was as sick as a pig, but not as sick as Maxwell was. Ha! Ha! Ha!

Wednesday June 3rd

Went to school today, couldn't concentrate, kept thinking about the stick insect. She has got lovely white teeth (straight of course). She made some jam tarts* for when I came home from school. She is not stingy* with the jam like some women are.

My father is smoking and drinking heavily, but he has been made temporarily* impotent according to Doreen. This is something I do not wish to know! Doreen talks to me as if I were another adult instead of her lover's son aged fourteen and two months and one day.

play-school *BE* a school for children who are between three and five years old **born out of wedlock** born when one's parents were not married **to extend** *here:* to continue with **tart** *G* Törtchen **stingy** *inf.* always being very unwilling to give s.th. **temporarily** for a short time

Thursday June 4th

Doreen answered the phone to my mother first thing this morning. My mother asked to speak to me. She demanded to know what Doreen was doing in the house. I told her that my father was having a breakdown and that Doreen Slater was looking after him. I told her about his redundancy*. I said he was drinking heavily, smoking too much and generally letting himself go. Then I went to school. I was feeling rebellious, so I wore red socks. It is strictly forbidden but I don't care any more.

Friday June 5th

Miss Sproxton spotted* my red socks in assembly! The old bag* reported me to pop-eyed Scruton. He had me in his office and gave me a lecture on the dangers of being a nonconformist*. Then he sent me home to change into regulation* black socks. My father was in bed when I got home; he was having his impotence cured. I watched *Play School** with Maxwell until he came downstairs. I told him about the sock saga*.

He instantly* turned into a raving loonie*! He phoned the school and dragged* Scruton out of a caretakers' strike-meeting. He kept shouting down the phone; he said, "My wife's left me, I've been made redundant, I'm in charge of an idiot boy",—Maxwell, I presume*—"and you're victimizing* my son because of the colour of his socks!" Scruton said if I came to school in black socks everything would be forgotten but my father said I would wear whatever colour socks I liked. Scruton said he was anxious* to maintain* standards. My father said that the England World Cup team in 1966 did not wear black socks, nor did Sir Edmund Hillary* in 1953. Scruton seemed to go quiet then. My father put the phone down. He said, "Round one to me".

This could well get into the papers: "Black socks row at school". My mother might read about it and come home.

redundancy [rɪ'dʌndənsɪ] being made unemployed **to spot** to notice **bag** *contempt.* old woman **nonconformist** s.o. who behaves in an unusual way **regulation** [ˌregjʊ'leɪʃn] a written rule **Play School** a British pre-school children's TV programme **saga** ['sɑːgə] *here:* a long story **instantly** at once **raving loonie** *sl.* a wild and mad person **to drag** to pull with difficulty **to presume** *here:* to think **to victimize** ['vɪktɪmaɪz] to treat s.o. very unfairly **to be anxious** ['æŋkʃəs] *here:* to wish strongly **to maintain** to keep up, to continue **Sir Edmund Hillary**/Tenzing Norgay: the first people to reach the top of Mount Everest in 1953

Saturday June 6th

Oh Joy! Oh Rapture*! Pandora is organizing a sock protest! She came round to my house today! Yes! She actually stood on our front porch* and told me that she admired the stand* I was taking! I would have asked her in, but the house is in a squalid state so I didn't. She is going round the school with a petition on Monday morning. She said I was a freedom fighter for the rights of the individual. She wants me to go round to her house tomorrow morning. A committee* is being set up, and I am the principal* speaker! She wanted to see the red socks but I told her they were in the wash.

Doreen Slater and Maxwell went home today. My grandma is coming round tonight, so all traces* of them have got to be wiped out.

Sunday June 7th
WHIT SUNDAY*

Grandma found Maxwell's dummy* in my father's bed. I lied and said that the dog must have brought it in off the street. It was a nasty moment. I am not a good liar, my face goes bright red and my grandma has got eyes like Superman's, they seem to bore right through you. To divert* her I told her about the red-sock row, but she said rules were made to be kept.

Pandora and the committee were waiting for me in the big lounge of her house. Pandora is Chairperson*, Nigel is Secretary and Pandora's friend Clair Neilson is Treasurer*. Craig Thomas and his brother Brett are just ordinary supporters. I am not allowed to hold high office because I am the victim*.

Pandora's parents were in the wooden kitchen doing *The Sunday Times* crossword. They seem to get on quite well together.

They brought a tray of coffee and health biscuits into the lounge for us. Pandora introduced me to her parents. They said they admired the stand that I was taking. They were both members of the Labour Party*

rapture *literary* great joy, happiness **porch** [pɔːtʃ] *here:* doorstep **stand** *here:* position, opinion **committee** [kəˈmɪtɪ] a small group of people who look after the interests of a larger group **principal** *here:* main **trace** [treɪs] a sign or mark **Whit Sunday** *G.* Pfingstsonntag **dummy** *BE G.* Schnuller **to divert s.o.** to make s.o. think of s.th. else **chairperson** s.o. who controls the meetings of a club, etc. **treasurer** [ˈtreʒərə] s.o. who looks after the money of a club **victim** *G.* Opfer **Labour Party** the main party for working class people and many middle class intellectuals in Britain

and they went on about the Tolpuddle Martyrs*. They asked me if the fact that I had chosen to protest in *red* socks had any significance*. I lied and said I had chosen red because it was a symbol of revolution, then I blushed* revolutionary red. I am turning into quite a liar recently.

Pandora's mother said I could call her Tania. Surely that is a Russian name? Her father said I could call him Ivan. He is very nice, he gave me a book to read; it is called *The Ragged Trousered Philanthropists**. I haven't looked through it yet but I'm quite interested in stamp collecting so I will read it tonight.

Washed red socks, put them on radiator to dry ready for the morning.

Monday June 8th

Woke up, dressed, put red socks on before underpants or vest. Father stood at the door and wished me luck. Felt like a hero. Met Pandora and rest of committee at corner of our road; all of us were wearing red socks. Pandora's were lurex. She has certainly got guts! We sang "We shall not be moved" all the way to school. I felt a bit scared when we went through the gates but Pandora rallied* us with shouts of encouragement*.

Pop-eyed Scruton must have been tipped off because he was waiting in the fourth-year cloakroom*. He was standing very still with his arms folded, staring with poached egg eyes. He didn't speak, he just nodded upstairs. All the red socks trooped* upstairs. My heart was beating dead loud. He went silently into his office and sat at his desk and started tapping his teeth with a school pen. We just stood there.

He smiled in a horrible way then rang the bell on his desk. His secretary came in, he said, "Sit down and take a letter, Mrs Claricoates". The letter was to our parents, it said:

Dear Mr and Mrs ....,

It is my sad duty to inform you that your son/daughter has deliberately* flaunted* one of the rules of this school. I take an extremely

Tolpuddle Martyrs ['tɒl,pʌdl 'mɑːtəz] six farmworkers who were sent to prison for forming a trade union (!) in the village of Tolpuddle in 1834 **significance** [sɪg'nɪfɪkəns] importance, meaning **to blush** to become red in the face **The Ragged Trousered Philanthropists** (1914) a novel by Robert Tressel about the problems of working class people (now a classic text for the labour movement) **philanthropist** [fɪ'lænθrəpɪst] s.o. who likes people and freely gives money to help them **philatelist** [fɪ'lætəlɪst] s.o. who likes collecting stamps **to rally** *here:* to cheer up **encouragement** giving hope **cloakroom** a room where one can leave coats, etc. **to troop** *inf.* to walk in a group **deliberate** [dɪ'lɪbərət] with a plan in mind **to flaunt** *here:* not to follow, to flout

serious view of this contravention*. I am therefore suspending* your son/daughter for a period of one week. Young people today often lack* sufficient* moral guidance* in the home, therefore I feel that it is my duty to take a firm stand in my school. If you wish to discuss the matter further with me do not hesitate to ring my secretary for an appointment.

Yours faithfully,
R. G. Scruton
Headmaster

Pandora started to say something about her O levels suffering but Scruton roared* at her to shut up! Even Mrs Claricoates jumped. Scruton said that we could wait until the letters had been typed, duplicated and signed and then we had better "hotfoot it* out of school". We waited outside Scruton's office. Pandora was crying (because she was angry and frustrated, she said). I put my arm round her a bit. Mrs Claricoates gave us our letters. She smiled very kindly, it can't be very easy working for a despot*.

We went round to Pandora's house but it was locked, so I said everyone could come round to my house. It was quite tidy for once, apart from the dog hairs. My father raged about* the letter. He is supposed to be a Conservative* but he is not being very conservative* at the moment.

I can't help* wishing that I had worn black socks on Friday.

Tuesday June 9th
MOON'S FIRST QUARTER

My father saw Scruton today and told him that if he didn't allow me back to school in whatever colour socks I like he would protest to his MP*. Mr Scruton asked my father who his MP was. My father didn't know.

contravention *fml. here:* forbidden action **to suspend s.o.** *here:* to forbid s.o. to come to school **to lack** to be without **sufficient** [sə'fɪʃnt] enough **guidance** help and advice **to roar** to shout out very loud **to hotfoot it** *inf.* to go very quickly **despot** ['despɒt] tyrant, dictator **to rage about** *here:* to talk angrily about **Conservative** a member of the Conservative Party **conservative** traditional *here: G.* zurückhaltend **can't help** *here:* can't avoid **MP** *BE short for:* Member of Parliament

Wednesday June 10th

Pandora and I are in love! It is official! She told Claire Neilson, who told Nigel, who told me.

I told Nigel to tell Claire to tell Pandora that I return her love. I am over the moon with joy and rapture. I can overlook the fact that Pandora smokes five Benson and Hedges a day and has her own lighter. When you are in love such things cease* to matter.

Thursday June 11th

Spent all day with my love. Can't write much, my hands are still trembling.

Friday June 12th

Had a message from the school to say that Bert Baxter wanted to see me urgently. Went round with Pandora (we are inseparable*). Bert is ill. He looked awful, Pandora made his bed up with clean sheets (she didn't seem to mind the smell) and I phoned the doctor. I described Bert's symptoms. Funny breathing, white face, sweating.

We tried to clean the bedroom up a bit, Bert kept saying stupid things that didn't make sense. Pandora said that he was delirious*. She held his hand until the doctor came. Dr Patel was quite kind, he said that Bert needed oxygen*. He gave me a number to ring for an ambulance, it seemed to take ages to come. I thought about how I had neglected Bert lately and I felt a real rat* fink*. The ambulancemen took Bert downstairs on a stretcher. They got stuck on the corner of the stairs and knocked a lot of empty beetroot jars over. Pandora and me cleared a path through the rubbish in the downstairs hall and they steered him through. He was wrapped* in a big, fluffy red blanket before he went outside. Then they shut him up in the ambulance and he was sirened away*. I had a big lump* in my throat and my eyes were watering. It must have been caused by the dust.

Bert's house is very dusty.

to cease [siːs] to stop **inseparable** always together **delirious** [dɪˈlɪrɪəs] mad with fever **oxygen** [ˈɒksɪdʒən] *G.* Sauerstoff **rat** *inf. contempt. here:* disloyal person **fink** *AE inf. contempt.* unpleasant person **to wrap** [ræp] to put cloth around **to siren s.o. away** to take s.o. away in an ambulance with its siren on **lump** *here: G.* Kloß

Saturday June 13th

Bert is in intensive care, he can't have visitors. I ring up every four hours to find out how he is. I pretend to be a relative. The nurses say things like "He is stable".

Sabre is staying with us. Our dog is staying at grandma's because it is scared of alsatians.

I hope Bert doesn't die. Apart from liking him, I have got nothing to wear to a funeral.

Still madly in love with P.

Sunday June 14th
TRINITY SUNDAY*

Went to see Bert, he has got tubes* all over him. I took him a jar of beetroot for when he is better. The nurse put it in his locker*. I took some "get well" cards, one from Pandora and me, one from my grandma, one from my father and one from Sabre.

Bert was asleep so I didn't stay long.

Monday June 15th

The Red Sock Committee has voted to give way to* Scruton for the time being*. We wear red socks underneath our black socks. This makes our shoes tight but we don't mind because a principle is involved*.

Bert has made a slight* improvement. He is awake more. I'll go round and see him tomorrow.

Tuesday June 16th

Bert has only got a few tubes left inside him now. He was awake when I went into his room. He didn't recognize me at first because I was wearing a mask and gown*. He thought I was a doctor. He said, "Get these bleedin'* tubes out of my private parts*, I ain't* an underground system".

Trinity Sunday the Sunday after Whit Sunday, one of the main festivals of the Christian year (*G.* Dreifaltigkeitsfest) **tube** *G.* Röhre **locker** a small cupboard or box with a lock **to give way to** *G.* nachgeben **for the time being** for now, until a better moment **to be involved** to be mixed up **slight** [slaɪt] *here*: small **gown** [gaʊn] *here: G.* Arztkittel **bleedin'/bleeding** (a swear word showing anger) **private parts** a polite word for: genitals **ain't** *very inf.* am not

Then he saw it was me and asked how Sabre was. We had a long talk about Sabre's behaviour problems, then the nurse came in and told me I had to go. Bert asked me to tell his daughters that he is on his deathbed; he gave me half-a-crown* for the phone calls! Two of them live in Australia! He said the numbers are written down in the back of his old army pay-book.

My father says that half-a-crown is roughly worth twelve and a half pence. I am keeping the half-a-crown. It has a nice chunky* feel about it and it will no doubt be a collector's item* one day.

Wednesday June 17th
FULL MOON

Pandora and me searched Bert's house looking for his army pay-book. Pandora found a pile of brown and cream postcards that were very indecent. They were signed "*avec tout mon amour chéri, Lola**". I felt a bit funny after looking through them, so did Pandora. We exchanged our first really passionate* kiss. I felt like doing a French kiss* but I don't know how it's done so I had to settle for* an ordinary English one.

No sign of the pay-book.

Thursday June 18th

Bert is now tubeless. He is being moved into an ordinary ward* tomorrow. I told him about not finding the army pay-book, he said it doesn't matter now he knows he's not dying.

Pandora came with me tonight. She got on well with Bert; they talked about Blossom. Bert passed on a few tips about grooming* ponies. Then Pandora went out to arrange the flowers she'd brought and Bert asked me if I'd had my "leg over" yet. Sometimes he is just a dirty old man who doesn't deserve* visitors.

Friday June 19th

Bert is on a big ward full of men with broken legs and bandaged chests. He looks a lot better now that he has got his teeth in. Some of the men

half-a-crown an English coin, not used any longer **chunky** ['tʃʌŋkɪ] *here:* heavy **item** ['aɪtəm] *here:* object, thing **avec tout mon amour chéri** *French for:* with all my love, darling **passionate** showing strong feelings **French kiss** *G.* Zungenkuss **to settle for s.th.** to accept s.th. **ward** [wɔːd] a room in a hospital or prison **to groom** to take care of horses **to deserve s.th.** to be worthy of s.th., to have a right to s.th.

whistled at Pandora when she walked down the ward. I wish she wasn't taller than me. Bert is in trouble with the ward sister for getting beetroot juice on the hospital sheets. He is supposed to be on a fluid* diet.

Saturday June 20th

I hope Bert can come home soon. My father is fed up with Sabre and my grandma is sick to death of our dog.

Bert's consultant* has told him to give up smoking but Bert says at eighty-nine years old it is hardly worth it. He has asked me to buy him twenty Woodbines and box of matches. What shall I do?

Sunday June 21st
FIRST AFTER TRINITY. FATHER'S DAY

Couldn't sleep last night for worrying about the Woodbines. After much heart-searching decided not to grant* Bert's wish. Then went to the hospital to find that Bert had bought his stinking* fags* from the hospital trolley*!

Just measured my thing. It has grown one centimetre. I might be needing it soon.

Monday June 22nd

Woke up with sore throat*, couldn't swallow*, tried to shout downstairs but could only manage a croak*. Tried to attract my father's attention by banging on my bedroom floor with school shoe but my father shouted, "Stop that bloody* banging". Eventually I sent the dog downstairs with a message tucked* inside its collar*. I waited for ages, then I heard the dog barking in the street. It hadn't delivered the message! I was close to despair*. I had to get up to go to the toilet but how I got there I don't know; it is all a hazy* blur*. I stood at the top of the stairs and croaked as loud as I could but my father had his Alma Cogan records on so I was forced to go downstairs and tell him I was ill. My father looked in my

fluid *G.* flüssig; Flüssigkeit **consultant** [kən'sʌltənt] a doctor in a hospital **to grant** *here:* to fulfil **stinking** *very inf. contempt.* extremely unpleasant **fags** *BE inf.* cigarettes **trolley** *here: G.* Verkaufswägelchen **sore throat** *G.* Halsschmerzen **to swallow** *G.* (hinunter)schlucken **to croak** to make a deep sound like that made by a frog **bloody** *BE* (swear word) **to tuck** *here:* to put, to push **collar** *here:* a band of leather, put around a dog's neck **despair** feeling of extreme hopelessness **hazy** ['heɪzɪ] misty, not clear **blur** s.th. that cannot be seen clearly

mouth and said, "Christ Almighty*, Adrian, your tonsils* look like Polaris missiles*! What are you doing down here? Get back into bed at once, you fool". He took my temperature: it was 112° Fahrenheit*. By rights* I should be dead.

It is now five minutes to midnight, the doctor is coming in the morning. I just pray that I can last out until then. Should the worst happen, I hereby leave all my wordly goods* to Pandora Braithwaite of 69 Elm Tree Avenue. I think I am of sound mind*. It is very hard to tell when you've got a temperature of 112° Fahrenheit.

Tuesday June 23rd

I have got tonsillitis*. It is official. I am on antibiotics. Pandora sits by my bed reading aloud to me. I wish she wouldn't, every word is like a rock dropping on my head.

Wednesday June 24th

A "get well" card from my mother. Inside a five-pound note. I asked my father to spend it on five bottles of Lucozade*.

Thursday June 25th
MOON'S LAST QUARTER

I have delirious dreams about Lady Diana Spencer*; I hope I am better in time for the wedding*. Temperature is still 112° Fahrenheit.

My father can't cope with* Sabre, so Pandora has taken him home with her. (Sabre, not my father.)

Friday June 26th

Doctor said our thermometer is faulty*. I feel slightly better.

Got up for twenty minutes today. Watched *Play School*; it was Carol Leader's turn, she is my favourite presenter.

Christ Almighty (swear word expressing surprise) **tonsils** *G.* Mandeln **Polaris missile** *G.* Polarisrakete (used by submarines) **112° Fahrenheit** about 44° Celsius **by rights** normally **wordly goods** *G.* weltliche Güter **to be of sound mind** *fml.* to be able to think clearly **tonsillitis** [ˌtɒnsɪˈlaɪtɪs] *G.* Mandelentzündung **Lucozade** (trademark) a sparkling, fizzy drink **Lady Diana Spencer** married Prince Charles in 1981 **wedding** marriage ceremony **to cope with s.th.** to deal with s.th. successfully **faulty** wrong, out of order

Pandora brought me a "get well" card. She made it herself with felt-tip pens. She signed it: "Forever yours, Pan."

I wanted to kiss her but my lips are still cracked*.

Saturday June 27th

Why hasn't my mother been to see me?

Sunday June 28th
SECOND AFTER TRINITY

My mother has just left to catch the train for Sheffield. I am worn out* with all the emotion. I am having a relapse*.

Monday June 29th

Pandora went to see Bert Baxter. She said the nurses are getting fed up with him because he won't stay in bed or do anything he is told to do. He is being discharged* on Thursday.

I long for the peace and quiet of a hospital ward. I would be a perfect patient.

Pandora's father has put Sabre into kennels, it is costing him three pounds a day, but Pandora's father says that it is worth every penny.

Tuesday June 30th

I am entering a period of convalescence*. I will have to take things very easily if I am to regain* my former vigour*.

Wednesday July 1st
DOMINION DAY*, CANADA. NEW MOON

The truant officer* came round this afternoon; he caught me sitting in a deckchair* in the front garden. He didn't believe I was ill! He is reporting me to the school! The fact that I was sipping* Lucozade whilst wear-

to crack to break **to be worn out** to feel extremely tired **relapse** *G.* Rückfall **to be discharged** *here:* to get sent home **convalescence** [ˌkɒnvəˈlesns] getting better, recovering **to regain** to get back **vigour** [ˈvɪgə] strength, energy **Dominion Day** celebration of the day in 1867 when Canada, a British colony, became a so-called dominion with a government of its own, but the Queen or King of England as its head of state **truant** [ˈtruːənt] **officer** an official who has to check why pupils are absent from school **deckchair** *G.* Liegestuhl **to sip** *G.* schlürfen, nippen

ing pyjamas, dressing gown* and slippers seemed to have escaped him. I offered to show him my yukky tonsils but he backed away and trod on the dog's paw. The dog has got a low pain threshold* so it went a bit berserk. My father came out and separated them but things could get nasty for us.

Thursday July 2nd

The doctor said I can go back to school tomorrow, depending on how I feel. You can depend that I won't feel up to it.

Friday July 3rd

A brown-skinned family are moving into Mr Lucas's old house! I sat in my deckchair and had a good view of their furniture being carried out of the removal van. The brown-skinned ladies kept taking massive cooking pots into the house so it looks as if they are a large family. My father said that it was "the beginning of the end of our street". Pandora is in the Anti-Nazi League*. She said she thinks that my father is a possible racist.

I am reading *Uncle Tom's Cabin**.

Saturday July 4th
INDEPENDENCE DAY*, USA

The street is full of brown-skinned people arriving or departing in cars, vans and mini-buses. They keep trooping in and out of Mr Lucas's old house. My father says they have probably got three families to each room.

Pandora and I are going round to welcome them to our district. We are determined to show that not all white people are racist fanatics.

Bert Baxter is still in hospital.

dressing gown [gaʊn] *G.* Bademantel, Morgenrock **pain threshold** *G.* Schmerzgrenze **Anti-Nazi League** [li:g] a group of people who are against Nazis **Uncle Tom's Cabin** an anti-slavery novel by H.B. Stowe (1852) **Independence Day** celebration of 4th July 1776, the day of the American Declaration of Independence (*G.* Tag der Unabhängigkeitserklärung)

Sunday July 5th
THIRD AFTER TRINITY

Stayed in bed until 6 p.m. There was no point in getting up. Pandora has gone to a gymkhana*.

Monday July 6th

Mrs O'Leary is trying to organize a street party for the Royal Wedding*. The only people to put their names down so far are the Singh family.

Tuesday July 7th

Bert Baxter has escaped from hospital. He telephoned the National Council for Civil Liberties* and they told him he could sign* himself out, so he did. He is in our spare room. My father is going up the wall.

Pandora, Bert and I have put our names down for the street party. Bert is looking much better now that he can smoke as many Woodbines as he likes.

Pandora's father has been round to talk to my father about what to do about Bert and Sabre. They both got drunk and started arguing about politics. Bert banged on the floor and asked them to keep their voices down*.

Wednesday July 8th

My father is near to despair because of Bert's snoring*. It doesn't bother me, I put Blu-tack* in my ears.

Went to school today. I have decided to take Domestic Science, Art, Woodwork and English O levels. I am doing Geography, Maths and History for CSE*.

Pandora is taking nine O levels. But she has had more advantages than me. She has been a member of the library since she was three.

gymkhana [dʒɪm'kɑːnə] meeting where riders show their skills **Royal Wedding** *here:* the marriage between Lady Diana and Prince Charles in 1981 **National Council for Civil Liberties** *G.* (brit.) Bürgerrechtsorganisation **to sign out** *here:* to leave the hospital officially **to keep one's voice down** to speak more quietly **to snore** to breathe noisily in one's sleep **Blu-tack** a blue plastic-like material, used to fasten posters, etc. to a wall **CSE** an examination taken at the age of 15, less difficult than GCE "O"-level which can be taken at the same age *(cf. p. 32)*

Thursday July 9th

School breaks up for eight weeks tomorrow. Pandora is going to Tunisia soon. How I will survive without my love is anybody's guess. We have tried French kissing but neither of us liked it, so we have gone back to the English.

My skin is dead good. I think it must be a combination of being in love and Lucozade.

Friday July 10th

It was magic at school toady. All the teachers were in good moods. A rumour* went round that pop-eyed Scruton was seen laughing but I didn't believe it myself.

Barry Kent climbed up the flagpole* and flew a pair of his mother's knickers in the breeze. Pandora said it was probably the first airing* they had had for years.

Sean O'Leary is nineteen today. He has invited me to his birthday party. It is only over the road so I won't have far to go.

I am writing up my diary now just in case I have one too many*. People seem to get drunk just stepping over the O'Leary's threshold*.

Saturday July 11th

First proper hangover*. Aged fourteen years, five months and nine days. Pandora put me to bed. She gave me a fireman's lift up the stairs.

Sunday July 12th
FOURTH AFTER TRINITY

My father took me, Pandora and Bert to the Wagtails boarding kennels* this morning. Mrs Kane, the proprietor*, has refused to keep Sabre any longer. It was very touching to see Bert and Sabre reunited*. Mrs Kane is a hard woman, she got very nasty when my father refused to pay Sabre's boarding fees*, she kept smoothing her black moustache* with her horny* fingers and using unladylike language.

rumour ['ru:mə] a report or story going from person to person **flagpole** *G.* Flaggenmast **airing** *G.* Lüften **to have one too many** to drink too much **threshold** *here: G.* Türschwelle **hangover** the unpleasant effects after drinking too much alcohol the night before **boarding kennels** *G.* Hundepension **proprietor** [prə'praɪətə] owner **to be reunited** to be together again **boarding fees** *G.* Pensionskosten **moustache** [mə'stɑ:ʃ] *G.* Schnurrbart **horny** having very hard skin

Bert said he won't be parted from* Sabre again. He said that Sabre is his only friend in the world! After all *I* have done for him!! If it wasn't for me he would be a corpse* by now, and Sabre would be an orphan* living with the RSPCA*.

Monday July 13th

Bert has been talking to Mrs Singh! He speaks fluent Hindi*! He says she has found some indecent magazines under the lino* in the bathroom. An heirloom* from that creep Lucas!

Mr Singh is outraged*. He has written to the estate agents to complain that his house has been defiled*.

Bert showed me one of the magazines. They are not indecent in my opinion, but then I am a man of the world. I have put it under my mattress with the *Big and Bouncys*. It is called *Amateur Photographer**.

Tuesday July 14th

Bert's social worker came round tonight. She is called Katie Bell. She talked to Bert in a stupid way. She said that Bert had been offered a place in the Alderman Cooper Sunshine Home. Bert told her that he didn't want to go. Katie Bell said that he has got to go. Even my father said that he felt sorry for Bert. But not sorry enough to invite Bert to live with us permanently I noticed!

Poor Bert, what will happen to him?

Wednesday July 15th

Bert has moved in with the Singhs. Mr Singh fetched Sabre's kennel so it is official. Bert looks dead happy. His favourite food is curry.

Pandora has allowed me to touch her bust. I promised not to tell anyone, but there was nothing to tell really. I couldn't tell where her bust began through all the layers* of underclothes, dress, cardigan and anorak.

I am reading *Sex, The Facts*, by Dr A. P. G. Haig.

to be parted from to be separated from **corpse** [kɔ:ps] the body of a dead person **orphan** ['ɔ:fn] a child whose parents are dead **RSPCA** *cf. p. 5* **Hindi** ['hɪndi:] one of the official languages of India **lino** *inf.* linoleum **heirloom** ['eəlu:m] *G.* Erbstück **to be outraged** to be extremely angry **to defile** ['di:faɪl] to make dirty, to pollute **Amateur Photographer** a monthly magazine for people who are interested in photography **layer** *G.* Schicht

Thursday July 16th

11 a.m. My father got his redundancy cheque* today. He did cowboy whoops* up and down the hall. He has asked Doreen Slater to go out with him to celebrate. Guess who Maxwell's baby sitter is going to be? Yes, dear diary, you guessed right! It is I!

11 p.m. Maxwell has only just gone to sleep, Pandora rang up at nine-thirty and asked how I was doing. I couldn't hear her properly because Maxwell was screaming so loudly. Pandora said I should try putting vodka in some hot milk and forcing it down his vile* throat. I have just done it. And it worked.

He is not a bad kid when he is asleep.

Friday July 17th
FULL MOON

My precious love leaves these shores tomorrow. I am going to the airport to see her off. I hope her plane won't suffer from metal fatigue*. I have just checked the world map to see where Tunisia is, and I am most relieved to see that Pandora won't have to fly through the Bermuda triangle*.

If anything happened to my love I would never smile again.

I have bought her a book to read during the flight. It is called *Crash!*, by a bloke called William Goldenstein, III. It is very good on what to do if the worst happens.

Saturday July 18th

Pandora read the *Crash!* book in the coach on the way to the airport. When her flight was called she had slight hysterics and her father had to carry her up the steps. I waved to the plane until it had retreated* into a large cloud, then I sadly got on a coach and came back home. How I will get through the next fortnight I don't know. Goodnight, my Tunisian beauty.

redundancy cheque cheque employers give to people whom they have made redundant (unemployed) **whoop** a loud and happy shout **vile** *contempt.* unpleasant **metal fatigue** [fə'ti:g] *G.* Materialermüdung **Bermuda Triangle** ['traɪæŋgl] the area between Bermuda, Florida, and Puerto Rico where many ships and planes have been lost **to retreat** to move back(wards), *here:* to disappear

Sunday July 19th
FIFTH AFTER TRINITY

Stayed in bed and looked at Tunisia on the map.

Monday July 20th

Not had a postcard from my love yet.

Tuesday July 21st

Bert came round this morning. He said that Tunisia is full of hazards*.

Wednesday July 22nd

Why haven't I had a postcard yet? What can have happened?

Thursday July 23rd

Asked our postman about communications between Tunisia and England. He said that they were "diabolical*"; he said that the Tunisian GPO* depends on camels.

Friday July 24th
MOON'S LAST QUARTER

Went to see Mr Singh. He said that Tunisia is very unhygienic. Everybody but me seems to be familiar with Tunisia!

Saturday July 25th

PANDORA! PANDORA! PANDORA!

Oh! my love,
My heart is yearning*,
My mouth is dry,
My soul is burning.
You're in Tunisia,
I am here.
Remember me and shed a tear*.
Come back tanned* and brown and healthy.
You're lucky that your dad is wealthy.

She will be back in six days.

hazard ['hæzəd] danger, risk **diabolical** [ˌdaɪə'bɒlɪkl] *inf. here:* extremely bad, dreadful **GPO** *here.* the Postal Service **to yearn** [jɜːn] to want very much **to shed a tear** to weep **tanned** *G.* braun gebrannt

Sunday July 26th

SIXTH AFTER TRINITY

Went for tea at grandma's. I was sad and withdrawn* because of Pandora's sojourn* in Tunisia. Grandma asked if I was constipated*. I nearly said something, but what's the use of trying to explain *love* to a woman of seventy-six who thinks the word is obscene?

Monday July 27th

A camel postcard! It said:

Dearest,

Economic* conditions here are quite dreadful. I was going to buy you a present but instead I gave all my money to a beggar*. You have such a generous heart Adrian that I feel sure you will understand. All my love into infinity*.

For ever,

Pandora X

Fancy* giving my present money to a filthy, idle* beggar! Even our postman was disgusted.

Tuesday July 28th

It's a wonder I have the strenght to hold my pen! I have been on the go* all day with preparations for the Royal Wedding street party. Mrs O'Leary came over and asked if I would help with the bunting*. I said "I feel it is my patriotic duty". Mrs O'Leary said that if I climbed the ladder she would pass the bunting up to me. I was all right for the first four or five rungs* but then I made the mistake of looking down and I had a vertigo* attack, so Mrs O'Leary did all the climbing. I couldn't help noticing Mrs O'Leary's knickers. They are surprisingly sexy for someone who goes to church every day and twice on Sundays. Black lace*! With red-satin ribbons*! I got the feeling that Mrs O'Leary knew that I was looking at her knickers because she asked me to call her Caitlin. I was glad

withdrawn shy, quiet **sojourn** ['sɒdʒɜːn] *fml.* stay **to be constipated** ['kɒnstɪpeɪtɪd] *G.* an Verstopfung leiden **economic** [ˌiːkə'nɒmɪk] *G.* ökonomisch, wirtschaftlich **beggar** s.o. who asks people for money or food **into infinity** *here:* without end **fancy!** *inf.* imagine! **idle** ['aɪdl] lazy, inactive **to be on the go** *inf.* to be busy **bunting** *G.* Fahnenschmuck **rung** *G.* Sprosse **vertigo** ['vɜːtɪgəʊ] a feeling of being sick, caused by looking down from a high place **lace** *G.* Spitze **ribbon** *G.* Band

when Mr O'Leary came to take over from me. Mr and Mrs Singh have hung a huge Union Jack* out of their front bedroom window. Bert told me that it was one he stole when he was in the army.

Our house is letting the street down*. All my father has done is pin a Charles and Diana tea towel to the front door.

My father and I watched the Royal Wedding firework display* on televison. All I can say is that I tried to enjoy it but failed. My father said it was one way of burning money. He is still bitter about being out of work.

I hope the Prince remembers to remove the price ticket off the bottom of his shoes; my father didn't at his wedding. Everyone in the church read the ticket. It said: "9 $^1/_2$ reject*, 10 shillings".

Wednesday July 29th

ROYAL WEDDING DAY!!!!!

How proud I am to be English!

Foreigners must be as sick as pigs!

We truly lead the world when it comes to pageantry*! I must admit to having tears in my eyes when I saw all the cockneys* who had stood since dawn*, cheering heartily all the rich, welldressed, famous people going by in carriages* and Rolls-Royces.

Grandma and Bert Baxter came to our house to watch the wedding because we have got a twenty-four-inch colour. They got on all right at first but then Bert remembered he was a communist and started saying anti-royalist* things like "the idle rich" and "parasites", so grandma sent him back to the Singhs' colour portable*.

Prince Charles looked quite handsome* in spite* of his ears. His brother is dead good-looking; it's a shame they couldn't have swapped* heads just for the day. Lady Diana melted my heartstrings* in her dirty white dress. She even helped an old man up the aisle*. I thought it was very kind of her considering* it was her wedding day. Loads of dead

Union Jack the national flag of the United Kingdom **to let s.o. down** to disappoint s.o. **display** show **reject** ['riː dʒekt] *here: G.* Ausschussware **pageantry** ['pædʒəntrɪ] *G.* Aufzug, Parade, Prachtentfaltung **cockney** s.o. who comes from East London, esp. a member of the working class **dawn** daybreak, first light of day **carriage** ['kærɪdʒ] *here: G.* Kutsche **anti-royalist** being against kings and queens **portable** a TV set that can be carried around **handsome** good-looking **in spite of** *G.* trotz **to swap** *G.* austauschen **to melt s.o.'s heartstrings** to make s.o. feel very emotional **aisle** [aɪl] *G.* Gang, Seitenschiff (einer Kirche) **considering** *G.* wenn man bedenkt, dass

famous people were there. Nancy Reagan*, Spike Milligan*, Mark Phillips*, etc., etc. The Queen looked a bit jealous. I expect it was because people weren't looking at *her* for a change.

The Prince had remembered to take the price ticket off his shoes. So that was one worry off my mind.

When the Prince and Di exchanged rings my grandma started to cry. She hadn't brought her handkerchief so I went upstairs to get the spare toilet roll. When I came downstairs they were married. So I missed the Historic moment of their marriage!

I made a cup of tea during all the boring musical interval, but I was back in time to see that Kiwi* woman singing. She has certainly got a good pair of lungs on her.

Grandma and I were just settling down to watch the happy couple's triumphant ride back to the palace when there was a loud banging on the front door. We ignored it so my father was forced to get out of bed and open the door. Bert and Mr and Mrs Singh and all the little Singhs came in asking for sanctuary*. Their telly* had broken down! My grandma tightened her lips, she is not keen on black, brown, yellow, Irish, Jewish* or foreign people. My father let them all in, then took grandma home in the car. The Singhs and Bert gathered round the television talking in Hindi.

Mrs Singh handed round some little Cornish pasties*. I ate one of them and had to drink a gallon* of water. I thought my mouth had caught fire! They were not Cornish pasties.

We watched televison until the happy couple left Victoria station* on a very strange-looking train. Bert said it was only strange-looking because it was clean.

Mrs O'Leary came in and asked if she could borrow our old chairs for the street party. In my father's absence I agreed and helped to carry them out on to the pavement*. Our street looked dead weird* without cars and with flags and bunting flapping about.

Mrs O'Leary and Mrs Singh swept the street clean. Then we all helped to put the tables and chairs out into the middle of the road. The women

Nancy Reagan wife of US president Ronald Reagan (1981–1989) **Spike Milligan** British comedian **Mark Phillips** the husband of Princess Anne, the daughter of Elizabeth II **Kiwi** *BE sl.* being from New Zealand **sanctuary** ['sæŋktjʊərɪ] *G.* Zuflucht, Asyl **telly** *inf.* television **Jewish** *G.* jüdisch **Cornish pasty** *BE G.* Blätterteig mit Fleischfüllung **gallon** *BE* 4.55 litres, *here:* a lot **Victoria Station** one of the main railway stations in London **pavement** a path at the side of the street for people to walk on **weird** [wɪəd] *BE inf.* unusual, strange

did all the work, the men stood around on the pavement drinking too much and making jokes about Royal Nuptials*.

Mr Singh put his stereo speakers out of his lounge windows and we listened to a Des O'Connor LP whilst we set the tables with sandwiches, jam tarts, sausage rolls* and sausages on sticks. Then everyone in our street was given a funny hat by Mrs O'Leary and we sat down to eat. At the end of the tea Mr Singh made a speech about how great it was to be British. Everyone cheered and sang "Land of Hope and Glory"*. But only Mr Singh knew all the words. Then my father came back with four party packs of light ale* and two dozen paper cups, and soon everyone was acting in an undignified* manner.

Mr O'Leary tried to teach Mrs Singh an Irish jig* but he kept getting tangled up in her sari*. I put my Abba LP on and turned the volume up high and soon even the old people of forty and over were dancing! When the street lamps came on Sean O'Leary climbed up and put red, white and blue crepe paper over the bulbs* to help the atmosphere and I fetched our remaining candles and put them on the tables. Our street looked quite Bohemian*.

Bert told some lies about the war, my father told jokes. The party went on until one o'clock in the morning!

Normally they get a petition up if you clear your throat after eleven o'clock at night!

I didn't dance, I was an amused, cynical* observer*. Besides my feet were aching*.

Thursday July 30th

I have seen the Royal Wedding repeats* seven times on television.

Friday July 31st
NEW MOON

Sick to death of Royal Wedding.

Pandora, the beggar's friend, is coming home tomorrow.

Royal Nuptials *fml. here:* Royal Wedding **sausage roll** *G.* Bratwurst im Schlafrock (Teig) **"Land of Hope ..."** a patriotic song about the British Empire (1902) **ale** a type of beer **undignified** foolish, embarrassing **Irish jig** an Irish dance **sari** ['sɑːrɪ] a piece of clothing worn by Indian women **bulb** *here: G.* Glühbirne **Bohemian** [bəʊ'hiːmjən] unconventional, different from ordinary people's life **cynical** ['sɪnɪkl] believing that people always act egoistically **observer** s.o. who watches **to ache** [eɪk] to hurt **repeat** *here: G.* Wiederholung

Saturday August 1st

Postcard from my mother, she wants me to go on holiday with her and creep Lucas. They are going to Scotland. I hope they enjoy themselves.

Pandora's flight has been delayed* because of a baggage-handlers' strike in Tunis.

Sunday August 2nd
SEVENTH AFTER TRINITY

The baggage-handlers are still on strike and Pandora's father has had his American Express card stolen by a beggar!

Pandora said that her mother has been bitten by a camel but is recovering in the Ladies' toilet at Tunis airport. It was wonderful to hear Pandora's voice on the telephone, we talked to each other for over half an hour. How clever it was of her to arrange a reverse-charge call* from Tunisia!

Monday August 3rd
BANK HOLIDAY IN SCOTLAND AND REP. OF IRELAND

The Tunisian baggage-handlers have agreed to go to arbitration*. Pandora says that with luck she'll be home by Thursday.

Tuesday August 4th

The Tunisian baggage-handlers can see light at the end of the tunnel*.

Pandora is surviving on packets of dates* and Polo mints.

Wednesday August 5th

The Tunisian baggage-handlers are now handling baggage. *Pandora home FRIDAY EVENING!*

Thursday August 6th

My father refused a reverse-charges call from Tunisia. Our lines of communication* have been cut.

to be delayed to be held up **reverse-charge call** a telephone call for which the person who gets the call has to pay **arbitration** [ˌɑːbɪˈtreɪʃn] *G.* Schlichtung(skommission) **to see the light at the end of the tunnel** *fig.* to see the end of a problem, to have hope **date** *here: G.* Dattel **line of communication** *here: G.* Verständigungsmöglichkeit

Friday August 7th
MOON'S FIRST QUARTER

I rang Tunisia whilst my father was in the bath. He shouted down to ask whom I was phoning. I told a lie. I said I was phoning the speaking clock.

Pandora's flight left safely. She should be home around midnight.

Saturday August 8th

At 7 a.m. Pandora rang from St Pancras* station. She said that due to* electrification* of the track at Flitwick she would be delayed.

I got dressed and went down to the station, got a platform ticket, waited on platform two for six cold, lonely hours. Went home to find a note from Pandora. This is what it said:

Adrian,
I confess* to feeling heartbroken at your apparent* coldness concerning my arrival. I felt sure that we would have an emotional reunion* on platform three. But it was not to be.
Adieu,
Pandora

Went to Pandora's house. Explained. Had an emotional reunion behind her father's tool shed.

Sunday August 9th
EIGHTH AFTER TRINITY

Touched Pandora's bust again. This time I think I felt something soft. My thing keeps growing and shrinking*, it seems to have a life of its own. I can't control it.

Monday August 10th

Pandora and I went to the swimming baths this morning. Pandora looked superb* in her white string bikini. She has gone the same colour as Mrs Singh. I didn't trust my thing to behave so I sat in the spectators'* gallery

St Pancras one of the main railway stations in London **due to** because of **electrification** [ɪˌlektrɪfɪ'keɪʃn] repairs making it possible to run trains by electricity **to confess** *here:* to admit **apparent** [ə'pærənt] easy to see **reunion** coming together again **to shrink** to become smaller **superb** excellent **spectator** s.o. who watches

and watched Pandora diving off the highest diving board. Got back to my house. Showed her my black room. Lit a joss stick. Put Abba LP on, sneaked* a bottle of Sanatogen* upstairs. We indulged* in a bit of light petting but then Pandora developed a headache and went home to rest.

I was racked with* sexuality but it wore off when I helped my father put manure* on our rose bed.

Tuesday August 11th

Got another postcard from my mother.

Dear Aidy,

You've no idea how much I long to see you. The mothering bond* is as strong as ever. I know you feel threatened* by my involvement* with Bimbo, but really Aidy there is no need. Bimbo fulfils my sexual needs. No more, no less. So, Aidy, grow up and came to Scotland.

Lots of love,

Pauline (mother)

P.S. We leave on the fifteenth. Catch 8.22 train to Sheffield.

The postman said that if my mother was his wife he would give her a good thrashing*. He doesn't know my mother. If anybody laid a finger on *her* she would beat them to pulp*.

Wednesday August 12th

Pandora thinks a trial* separation* will do us good. She says our light to medium petting will turn quite heavy soon. I must admit that the strain* is having a detrimental* effect on my health. I have got no energy and my sleep is constantly interrupted with dreams about Pandora's white bikini and Mrs O'Leary's knickers.

I might go to Scotland after all.

to sneak s.th. to take s.th. secretly **Sanatogen** (trademark) name of a tonic wine (*G.* Stärkungswein) **to indulge** [ɪn'dʌldʒ] **in** to give way to one's wishes **to be racked with** *here:* to suffer from **manure** [mə'njʊə] *G.* Dung, Mist **bond** a strong feeling between two people **to threaten** *G.* bedrohen **involvement** *here:* (sexual) relationship **to give s.o. a thrashing** *inf.* to beat s.o. **to beat s.o. to pulp** *inf. G.* jemanden zu Brei schlagen **trial** ['traɪəl] *here:* test **separation** [ˌsepə'reɪʃn] *here:* not being together **strain** pressure, stress **detrimental** [ˌdetrɪ'mentl] damaging, harmful

Thursday August 13th

My father has decided to go to Skegness on the fifteenth. He has booked a four-berth* caravan. He is taking Doreen and Maxwell with him! He expects me to go!

If I go people will automatically assume* that Doreen is my mother and Maxwell is my brother!

I am going to Scotland.

Friday August 14th

Had tragic last night with Pandora. We have both sworn to be true. I have done all my packing. The dog has been taken round to grandma's with fourteen tins of Pedigree Chum and a giant* sack of Winalot.

I am taking *Escape from Childhood*, by John Holt, to read on the train.

Saturday August 15th
FULL MOON

My father, Stick Insect and Maxwell House saw me off* at the station. My father didn't mind a bit that I chose to go to Scotland instead of Skegness. In fact he looked dead cheerful. The train journey was terrible. I had to stand all the way to Sheffield. I spoke to a lady in a wheelchair* who was in the guard's* van*. She was very nice, she said that the only good thing about being handicapped was that you always got a seat in trains. Even if it *was* in the guard's van.

My mother and creep Lucas met me at Sheffield. My mother looked dead thin and has started dressing in clothes that are too young for her. Lucas creep was wearing jeans! His belly* was hanging over his belt. I pretended to be asleep until we got to Scotland.

Lucas mauled* my mother about even whilst he was driving.

We are at a place called Loch Lubnaig*. I am in bed in a log cabin*. My mother and Lucas have gone to the village to try to buy cigarettes. At least that is their story.

berth [bɜ:θ] *here:* bed **to assume** to suppose, to think **giant** ['dʒaɪənt] huge, very big **to see s.o. off** to say good-bye to s.o. **wheelchair** *G.* Rollstuhl **guard** *here:* s.o. whose job it is to check train tickets **van** *here: G.* Waggon, Wagen **belly** *BE inf.* the part of the body where the stomach is **to maul** *here:* to touch s.o. roughly and in a sexual way **loch** [lɒk] (a word used in Scotland) lake **Loch Lubnaig** name of a lake in central Scotland **log cabin** a small house, made of thick pieces of wood

Sunday August 16th
NINTH AFTER TRINITY

There is a loch in front of the cabin and a pine forest and a mountain behind the cabin. There is nothing to do. It is dead boring.

Monday August 17th

Did some washing in a log cabin launderette*. Spoke to an American tourist called Hamish Mancini; he is the same age as me. His mother is on her honeymoon* for the fourth time.

Tuesday August 18th

Rained all day.

Wednesday August 19th

Sent postcards. Phoned Pandora, reversed charges. Her father refused to accept them.

Thursday August 20th

Played cards with Hamish Mancini. His mother and stepfather and my mother and her lover have gone to see a waterfall in the car. Big deal!

Friday August 21st

Walked two and a half miles into Callander* to buy Mars bar. Played on Space Invaders*. Came back, had tea. Phoned Pandora from log cabin phone box. Reversed charges. She still loves me. I still love her. Went to bed.

Saturday August 22nd
MOON'S LAST QUARTER

Went to see Rob Roy's* grave. Saw it, came back.

launderette [ˌlɔːndəˈret] a shop where people can use washing-machines **honeymoon** the holiday of a man and a woman who have just married **Callander** name of a small town near Loch Lubnaig, north-west of Stirling **Space Invaders** a computer video game **Rob Roy** (1671–1734) a Scotsman who fought against the English and was made the hero of a famous novel by Sir Walter Scott (1817)

Sunday August 23rd
TENTH AFTER TRINITY

My mother has made friends with a couple called Mr and Mrs Ball. They have gone off to Stirling* Castle. Mrs Ball has got a daughter who is a writer. I asked her how her daughter qualified to be one. Mrs Ball said that her daughter was dropped on her head as a child and has been "a bit queer*" ever since.

It is Mrs Ball's birthday so they all came back to our log cabin to celebrate. I complained about the noise at 1 a.m., 2 a.m., 3 a.m., and 4 a.m. At 5 a.m. they decided to climb the mountain! I pointed out to them that they were blind drunk*, too old, unqualified, unfit and lacking in any survival* techniques, had no first-aid kit*, weren't wearing stout* boots, and had no compass, map or sustaining* hot drinks.

My protest fell on deaf ears. They all climbed the mountain, came down and were cooking eggs and bacon by 11.30 a.m.

As I write Mr and Mrs Ball are canoeing on the loch. They must be on drugs.

Monday August 24th

Went to Edinburgh*. Saw the castle, the toy museum, the art gallery. Bought a haggis*. Came back to log cabin, read *Glencoe**, by John Prebble*. We are going there tomorrow.

Tuesday August 25th

The massacre of Glencoe took place on February 13, 1692. On February 14, John Hill wrote to the Earl of Tweeddale, "I have ruined Glencoe".

He was dead right, there is nothing there. Glasgow* tomorrow.

Stirling a town in central Scotland (about 29,000 people) **queer** *inf.* funny, strange **blind drunk** *inf.* very drunk **survival** *here: G.* Überlebens- **first-aid kit** *G.* Verbandskasten, Erste-Hilfe-Kasten **stout** [staʊt] strong **to sustain** [sə'steɪn] *here:* to give energy, to keep going **Edinburgh** the capital of Scotland, often called "Athens of the North" (about 475,000 people) **haggis** ['hægɪs] *G.* schottisches Nationalgericht: eine Art Wurst mit einer Hülle aus Schafsmagen, gefüllt mit Innereien und Haferschrot **Glencoe** a place in West Scotland where 38 members of the Macdonald Clan were brutally murdered by a rival family and English troops (1692) **John Prebble** a writer of books on Scottish history **Glasgow** a city and port in central Scotland (about 897,000 people) with one of the finest British museums

Wednesday August 26th

We drove through Glasgow at 11 a.m., in the morning yet I counted twenty-seven drunks in one mile! All the shops except the DIY shops had grilles at the windows. Off-licences* had rolls of barbed wire* and broken glass on their roofs. We had a walk round for a bit, then my mother nagged Lucas creep into taking her to the Glasgow art gallery. I intended to sit in the car and read *Glencoe*, but because of all the drunks staggering around I reluctantly* followed them inside.

How glad I am that I did! I might have gone through life without having an important cultural experience!

Today I saw Salvador Dali's* painting of the Crucifixion*!!! *The real one!* Not a reproduction!

They have hung it at the end of a corridor so that it changes as you get nearer to it. When you are finally standing up close to it you feel like a midget. It is absolutely fantastic!

Huge! With dead good colours and Jesus looks like a real bloke. I bought six postcards of it from the museum but of course it is not the same as the real thing.

One day I will take Pandora to see it. Perhaps on our honeymoon.

Thursday August 27th

Oban* today. Bumped into* Mr and Mrs Swallow who live in the next street to me. Everyone kept saying, "It's a small world isn't it?" Mrs Swallow asked creep Lucas how his wife was. Lucas told her that his wife had left him for another woman. Then everyone blushed and said what a small world it was and parted company*. My mother went mad at Lucas. She said "Do you have to tell everyone?" and "How do you think I feel living with a lesbian's estranged husband*?" Lucas whined on for a bit but then my mother started looking like my grandma. So he kept quiet.

off-licence *BE* a shop that sells alcohol to take away **barbed wire** *G.* Stacheldraht **reluctant** [rɪˈlʌktənt] unwilling **Salvador Dali** a Spanish painter (1904–1989) **crucifixion** [ˌkruːsɪˈfɪkʃn] nailing s.o. to a cross (Dali's painting is about the crucifixion of Christ) **Oban** [ˈəʊbən] a town and port in West Scotland **to bump into** *inf.* to meet **to part company** to go in different directions **estranged** [ɪˈstreɪnʒd] **husband** a husband who does not live with his wife any longer

Friday August 28th

Fort William* today. Ben Nevis* was another disappointment. I couldn't tell where it began or stopped. The other mountains and hills clutter it up*. Lucas fell in the burn (Scottish for "little river") but unfortunately it was too shallow to drown in.

Saturday August 29th
FULL MOON

Went for a walk around the loch with Hamish Mancini. He told me that he thinks his mother is heading for her fourth divorce. He is going home tonight; he has got an appointment with his analyst* in New York on Monday morning.

I have finished my packing and I am waiting for my mother and creep Lucas to come back from their furtive* love-making somewhere in the pine* forest.

We leave at dawn.

Sunday August 30th
ELEVENTH AFTER TRINITY

I made Lucas stop for souvenirs at Gretna Green*. I bought Pandora a pebble shaped like an otter, Bert a tam-o'-shanter*, the dog a tartan* bow* for its neck, grandma a box of tartan fudge*, Stick Insect tartan biscuits, Maxwell a tartan sweet dummy. I bought my father a tartan tea towel.

I bought myself a tartan scribbling pad*. I am determined* to become a writer.

Here is an extract from "My thoughts on Scotland" written on the M*6 at 120 mph:

The hallowed* mist rolls away leaving Scotland's majestic peaks*

Fort William a town in West Scotland **Ben Nevis** the highest mountain in Britain (1343 m), situated near Fort William **to clutter s.th. up** *here: G.* verdecken **analyst** ['ænəlɪst] *here:* psychoanalyst **furtive** ['fɜːtɪv] secret **pine** *G.* Kiefer **Gretna Green** a village in South Scotland where English people could be married without the usual formalities until 1940 **tam-o'-shanter** a Scottish flat wool cap with a bobble on top **tartan** ['tɑːtən] *G.* Schottenmuster, -karo **bow** *here: G.* Schleife **fudge** [fʌdʒ] a brown sweet made from sugar, milk and butter **scribbling pad** *G.* Notizblock **determined** [dɪ'tɜːmɪnd] having made up one's mind **M** *BE short for:* motorway **hallowed** ['hæləʊd] respected **peak** *here:* the top of a mountain

revealed* in all their majesty. A shape in the translucent* sky reveals itself to be an eagle, that majestic bird of prey*. Talons* clawing*, it lands on a loch, rippling the quiet majesty of the turbulent waters. The eagle pauses only to dip its majestic beak* into the aqua* before spreading its majestic wings and flying away to its magisterial* nest high in the barren*, arid*, grassless hills.

The Highland cattle*. Majestic horned beast of the glens* lowers its brown eyed shaggy haired majestic head as it ruminates* on the mysteries of Glencoe.

There are a couple too many "majestics". But I think it reads rather well. I will send it to the BBC when it's finished. Got home at 6 p.m. Too tired to write more.

Monday August 31st

BANK HOLIDAY IN UK (EXCEPT SCOTLAND)

Everyone is broke*. The banks are closed and my father can't remember the secret code on his plastic moneycard. He had the nerve to borrow five pounds from Bert Baxter. Fancy asking an old age pensioner for money! It lacks dignity*.

Pandora and I are now insanely* in love! The separation only served to fuel* our passion. Our hormones are stirred* every time we meet. Pandora slept with the otter pebble in her hand last night. How I wish the otter pebble could have been me.

Tuesday September 1st

Mr Singh has had to return to India to look after his aged parents, so Bert has been told that he will have to move back into his dirty old house! Mr Singh says that he cannot trust* his womenfolk* to be alone in the house with Bert. How stupid can you get? Bert doesn't mind too much; he said that it is "quite a compliment".

Pandora and I are going to clean Bert's house and help him move back.

to reveal *here:* to make visible **translucent** [trænz'lu:snt] allowing light to pass through **bird of prey** [preɪ] a bird that hunts other animals for food **talon** ['tælən] *G.* Kralle, Klaue **to claw** *G.* krallen **beak** the hard part of a bird's mouth **aqua** *Latin* water **magisterial** [ˌmædʒɪ'stɪrɪəl] commanding, producing respect **barren** dry, unproductive **arid** ['ærɪd] dry **cattle** i.e. cows and bulls **glen** a valley in the Scottish mountains **to ruminate** ['ru:mɪneɪt] *fml.* to think about s.th. carefully **broke** *inf.* having no money left **dignity** *G.* Würde **insane** [ɪn'seɪn] mad **to fuel** [fjʊəl] *here:* to make stronger **to stir** to move **to trust** *G.* (ver)trauen **womenfolk** women

He owes the council two hundred and ninety-four pounds in rent arrears*. He has got to pay the arrears off at fifty pence a week, so it is a certainty that Bert will die in debt.

Wednesday September 2nd

Pandora and I went to look at Bert's house today. It is a truly awesome* sight. If Bert took all his empty beer bottles back to the off-licence he might get enough money on the empties* to pay off his rent arrears.

Thursday September 3rd

My father helped us to move all of the furniture out of the ground floor of Bert's house, the woodworms came out to sunbathe. When we lifted the carpets we discovered that Bert had been walking about on a layer* of dirt, old newspapers, hairpins, marbles* and decomposed* mice for years. We hung the carpets on the washing line and beat them all afternoon, but the dust billowed* out non-stop. Pandora got excited at about 5 p.m., she claimed she could see a pattern* emerging* on one carpet, but closer examination showed it to be squashed* fairy cake*. We are going back tomorrow with Pandora's mother's carpet-shampooer. Pandora said it has been tested by *Which**?, but I bet it has never had to clean a filthy hovel* like Bert Baxter's before.

Friday September 4th

I have just witnessed* a miracle*! This morning Bert's carpets were dark grey in colour. Now one is a red Axminster* and the other is a blue Wilton*. The carpets are hanging on the clothes line to dry. We have scraped all the floors clean and washed the furniture down with a fungicide* disinfectant. Pandora took the curtains down but they fell to pieces before she could get them to the sink. Bert has been sitting in a deckchair criticizing and complaining. He can't see what's wrong with living in a dirty house.

What *is* wrong with living in a dirty house?

rent arrears [ə'rɪəz] *G.* Mietrückstände **awesome** ['ɔ:səm] causing a feeling of respect and fear **empties** *inf.* empty bottles **layer** *G.* Schicht **marble** *here: G.* Murmel **to decompose** [ˌdi:kəm'pəʊz] to break up, to rot **to billow** to rise and roll in waves **pattern** *G.* Muster **to emerge** [ɪ'mɜ:dʒ] to come to light **to squash** to make s. th. flat, to crush **fairy cake** a small cake **Which?** *cf.* the German magazine "Test" **hovel** *G.* Bruchbude, Loch **to witness** to see s. th. happen **miracle** ['mɪrəkl] a wonderful and surprising event **Axminster/Wilton** trademarks for British carpets **fungicide** ['fʌndʒɪsaɪd] *G.* pilztötend

Saturday September 5th

My father took Bert's bottles to the off-licence this morning. The boot, back seat and floor of the car were filled with them. The car stank of brown ale. He ran out of petrol on the way and called the AA*. The AA man was most uncivil, he said it wasn't the Automobile Association my father needed, it was Alcoholics Anonymous!

Sunday September 6th

TWELFTH AFTER TRINITY. MOON'S FIRST QUARTER

Bert's house looks great. Everything is dead clean and shiny. We have moved his bed into the lounge so that he can watch television in bed. Pandora's mother has done very artistic* arrangements with flowers, and Pandora's father has made an alsatian flap* in the back door so that Bert doesn't keep having to get up to answer the door to Sabre.

Bert is moving back tomorrow.

Monday September 7th

LABOR* DAY, USA AND CANADA

An airmail letter from Hamish Mancini.

> Hi Aid!
>
> Howya doin'*? I hope the situation Pandora-wise* is ongoing! She sounds kinda* zappy*! Scotland blew my mind! It was so far out as to be nuked*! You're a great human being, Aid. I guess I was kinda traumatized* when we rapped* but Dr Eagelburger (my shrink*) is doing great things with my libido*. Mom's really wiped out* right now, turns out number four is a TV* and has a better collection of Calvin Kleins* than she do! Don't you think the fall* is a drag? Son-of-a-bitch* leaves everywhere!
>
> See you, Buddy*!!!
>
> Hamish

AA *short for:* Automobile Association *cf.* the German ADAC **artistic** *G.* künstlerisch **flap** *G.* Klappe **Labor** *AE* labour *(BE)*, hard work **Howya doin'** *AE sl.* how are you? **Pandora-wise** *AE inf.* concerning Pandora **kinda** *very inf.* kind of **zappy** *inf.* energetic, dynamic **It was so far out as to be nuked.** *G.* etwa: Es war unglaublich irre. **to traumatize** to shock **to rap** *AE sl.* to talk freely **shrink** *humorous for:* psychoanalyst **libido** [lɪ'bi:dəʊ] *here:* sexual desire **wiped out** *AE sl.* excited **TV** *here: short for:* transvestite **Calvin Kleins** *here:* clothes designed by the American Calvin Klein **fall** *AE* autumn *(BE)* **son-of-a-bitch** *sl.* (a swear word) **buddy** *inf.* friend

I showed it to Pandora, my father and Bert but nobody understands it. Bert doesn't like Americans because it took them too long to come into the war or something.

Bert now in his clean house. He hasn't said thank-you, but he seems happy.

Tuesday September 8th

Lousy* stinking school on Thursday. I tried my old uniform on but I have outgrown it so badly that my father is being forced to buy me a new one tomorrow.

He is going up the wall but I can't help it if my body is in a growth* period can I? I am only five centimetres shorter than Pandora now. My thing remains static at twelve centimetres.

Wednesday September 9th

Grandma phoned, she has found out about Doreen and Maxwell going to Skegness. She is never speaking to my father again.

Here is my shopping list:

Blazer	£ 29.99
2 pairs grey trousers	£ 23.98
2 white shirts	£ 11.98
2 grey pullovers	£ 7.98
3 pairs black socks	£ 2.37
1 pair PE shorts	£ 4.99
1 PE vest*	£ 3.99
1 track suit	£ 11.99
1 pair training shoes	£ 7.99
1 pair football boots and studs*	£ 11.99
1 pair football socks	£ 2.99
Football shorts	£ 4.99
Football shirt	£ 7.99
Adidas sports bag	£ 4.99
1 pair black shoes	£ 15.99
1 calculator	£ 6.99
Pen and pencil set	£ 3.99
Geometry set	£ 2.99

lousy *inf. contempt.* bad, rotten **growth** *G.* Wachstum **vest** *(BE) G.* Unterhemd
stud *G.* (Fußballschuh:) Stollen

My father can easily spare* a hundred pounds. His redundancy payment must have been huge, so why he is lying on his bed moaning* I don't know. He is just a mean skinflint*! He hasn't paid with *real* money anyway! He used his American Express card.

Pandora admired me in my new uniform. She says she thinks I stand a good chance of being made a prefect*.

Thursday September 10th

A proud start to the new term. I am a prefect! My first duty is as late duty prefect. I have to wait by the gap in the railings and take the name of anyone sneaking late into school. Pandora is also a prefect. She is in charge of silence in the dinner queue.

My new timetable was given to me today by my new form tutor*, Mr Dock. It includes my O level and CSE lessons, and it is compulsory* to do Maths, English, PE and Comparative* Religion. But they do give you a choice of Cultural and Creative subjects. So I have chosen Media Studies (dead easy, just reading newspapers and watching telly) and Parentcraft (just learning about sex, I hope). Mr Dock also teaches English Literature, so we are bound to* get on, by now I am surely the best-read kid in the school. I will be able to help him out if he gets stuck*.

Asked my father for five pounds fifty for school trip to the British Museum. He went berserk and said, "What happened to free education?" I told him that I didn't know.

Friday September 11th

Had a long talk with Mr Dock. I explained that I was a one-parent-family child with an unemployed, bad-tempered* father. Mr Dock said he wouldn't care if I was the offspring* of a black, lesbian, one-legged mother and an Arab, leprous, humpbacked*-dwarf* father so long as my essays were lucid*, intelligent and unpretentious*. So much for pastoral care*!

to spare *here:* to give **to moan** [məʊn] to make a low and miserable sound **mean skinflint** *inf., contempt.* s.o. who hates spending money **prefect** an older pupil with special duties who helps teachers to control pupils **form tutor** *cf.* our German "Klassenlehrer" **compulsory** [kəm'pʌlsərɪ] obligatory **comparative** [kəm'pærətɪv] *here: G.* vergleichend **to be bound to do s.th.** to be certain to do s.th. **to get stuck** not to be able to go on **bad-tempered** angry **offspring** *here:* child, son **humpbacked** (=hunchbacked) *G.* buckelig **dwarf** [dwɔ:f] an unusually small person **lucid** ['lu:sɪd] very clear **unpretentious** [ˌʌnprɪ'tenʃəs] simple, modest **pastoral care** *G.* Seelsorge

Saturday September 12th

Wrote lucid, intelligent and unpretentious essay about Scottish wild life in the morning. In afternoon did shopping in Sainsbury's with my father. Saw Rick Lemon dithering* at the fruit counter; he said selecting* fruit was an "overtly* political act". He rejected* South African apples, French golden delicious apples, Israeli oranges, Tunisian dates, and American grapefruits. In the end he selected English rhubarb, "Although", he said, "the shape was phallic*, possibly sexist*". His girlfriend, Tit (short for Titia), was cramming* the trolley with pulses* and rice. She had a long skirt on but now and again I caught a glimpse* of her hairy ankles. My father said he preferred a nice shaven leg any day. My father likes stockings, suspenders*, mini-skirts and low necklines! He is dead old-fashioned.

Sunday September 13th

THIRTEENTH AFTER TRINITY

Went to see Blossom. Pandora doesn't ride her now because her feet drag on the ground. Pandora is having a proper horse delivered next week. It is called Ian Smith*. The people who are selling it used to live in Africa, in Zimbabwe.

Tomorrow is my mother's birthday. She is thirty-seven.

Monday September 14th

FULL MOON

Phoned my mother before school. There was no answer. I expect she was lying in bed with that stinking rat Lucas.

School dinners are complete crap* now. Gravy seems to have been phased out* along with custard and hot puddings. A typical menu is: hamburger, baked beans, chips, carton of yoghurt, or a doughnut*. It's not enough to build healthy bone and sinew*. I am considering making

to dither ['dɪðə] to hesitate **to select** to choose **overt** ['əʊvɜːt] open to view, obvious **to reject** [–'–] to say "no" to **phallic** ['fælɪk] like a penis **sexist** *here:* believing that women are less able than men, treating women unfairly in words or actions **to cram** to fill s. th. too full **pulse** *here:* beans, peas, etc. **glimpse** a quick look **suspender** a fastening which holds a woman's stockings up **Ian Smith** until 1979 prime minister of Rhodesia (now called Zimbabwe) when only white people had all the power there **crap** *inf. very unfriendly* useless object, junk **to phase out** to take away bit by bit **doughnut** ['dəʊnʌt] a small round cake, filled with jam (G. Berliner) **sinew** ['sɪnjuː] *fml.* muscle

a protest to Mrs Thatcher. It won't be our fault if we grow up apathetic* and lacking in moral fibre*. Perhaps Mrs Thatcher wants us to be too weak to demonstrate in years to come.

Tuesday September 15th

Barry Kent has been late three times in one week. So it is my unfortunate duty to report him to Mr Scruton.

Unpunctuality is the sign of a disordered* brain. So he cannot go unpunished.

Wednesday September 16th

Our form is going to the British Museum* on Friday. Pandora and I are going to sit together on the coach. She is bringing her *Guardian* from home so that we can have some privacy.

Thursday September 17th

Had a lecture on the British Museum from Ms Fossington-Gore. She said it was a "fascinating treasure* house of personkind's* achievements*". Nobody listened to the lecture. Everyone was watching the way she felt her left breast whenever she got excited.

Friday September 18th

2 a.m. Just got back from London. Coach driver suffered from motorway madness on the motorway. I am too shaken by the experience to be able to give a lucid or intelligent account* of the day.

Saturday September 19th

The school may well want a clear account by an unprejudiced* observer of what happened on the way to, during and coming back from our trip to London. I am the only person qualified. Pandora, for all her qualities, does not possess my nerves of steel.

apathetic [ˌæpəˈθetɪk] not interested in anything **moral fibre** [ˈfaɪbə] moral strength **disordered** *here:* sick **British Museum** a famous museum in London (built in 1753) with one of the world's richest collections in antiquities **treasure** [ˈtreʒə] *G.* Schatz **personkind** *usually:* mankind (*G.* Menschheit) – Adrian's teacher here wants to avoid sexist language **achievement** [əˈtʃiːvmənt] *G.* Leistung **account** *here:* report **unprejudiced** [ˌʌnˈpredʒʊdɪst] without unfair feelings

Class Four-D's Trip to the British Museum

7 a.m. Boarded* coach.

7.05 Ate packed lunch, drank low-calorie drink.

7.10 Coach stopped for Barry Kent to be sick.

7.20 Coach stopped for Claire Neilson to go to the Ladies.

7.30 Coach left school drive*.

7.35 Coach returned to school for Ms Fossington-Gore's handbag.

7.40 Coach driver observed to be behaving oddly*.

7.45 Coach stopped for Barry Kent to be sick again.

7.55 Approached motorway.

8.00 Coach driver stopped coach and asked everyone to stop giving "V" signs to lorry drivers.

8.10 Coach driver loses temper, refuses to drive on motorway until "bloody teachers control kids".

8.20 Ms Fossington-Gore gets everyone sitting down.

8.25 Drive on to motorway.

8.30 Everyone singing "Ten Green Bottles".

8.35 Everyone singing "Ten Green Snotrags"*.

8.45 Coach driver stops singing by shouting very loudly.

9.15 Coach driver pulls in at service station and is observed to drink heavily from hip-flask*.

9.30 Barry Kent hands round bars of chocolate stolen from self-service shop at service station. Ms Fossington-Gore chooses Bounty bar.

9.40 Barry Kent sick in coach.

9.50 Two girls sitting near Barry Kent are sick.

9.51 Coach driver refuses to stop on motorway.

9.55 Ms Fossington-Gore covers sick in sand.

9.56 Ms Fossington-Gore sick as a dog.

10.30 Coach crawls along on hard shoulder*, all other lanes* closed for repairs.

11.30 Fight breaks out on back seat as coach approaches end of motorway.

11.45 Fight ends. Ms Fossington-Gore finds first-aid kit and sees to wounds. Barry Kent is punished by sitting next to driver.

11.50 Coach breaks down at Swiss Cottage*.

to board *G.* einsteigen **drive** *G.* Einfahrt, Zufahrt **odd** *here:* strange **snotrag** sl. handkerchief (snot *G.* Rotz) **hip-flask** a small metal container for brandy, whisky, etc. **hard shoulder** *BE here: G.* Standstreifen, Seitenstreifen **lane** *here:* one of the parallel parts into which wide roads are divided (*G.* Fahrspur) **Swiss Cottage/Bloomsbury/ Soho** different parts of London

11.55 Coach driver breaks down in front of AA man.

12.30 Class Four-D catch London bus to St Pancras.

1 p.m. Class Four-D walk from St Pancras through Bloomsbury.

1.15 Ms Fossington-Gore knocks on door of Tavistock House, asks if Dr. Laing* will give Barry Kent a quick going-over. Dr Laing in America on lecture tour.

1.30 Enter British Museum. Adrian Mole and Pandora Braithwaite awestruck* by evidence of heritage* of World Culture. Rest of class Four-D run berserk, laughing at nude statues and dodging* curators*.

2.15 Ms Fossington-Gore in state of collapse. Adrian Mole makes reverse-charge phone call to headmaster. Headmaster in dinner lady strike-meeting, can't be disturbed.

3 p.m. Curators round up class Four-D and make them sit on steps of museum.

3.05 American tourists photograph Adrian Mole saying he is a "cute* English schoolboy".

3.15 Ms Fossington-Gore recovers* and leads class Four-D on sightseeing tour of London.

4 p.m. Barry Kent jumps in fountain* at Trafalgar Square, as predicted* by Adrian Mole.

4.30 Barry Kent disappears, last seen heading towards* Soho.

4.35 Police arrive, take Four-D to mobile police unit*, arrange coach back. Phone parents about new arrival time. Phone headmaster at home. Claire Neilson has hysterical fit*. Pandora Braithwaite tells Ms Fossington-Gore she is a disgrace* to teaching profession*. Ms Fossington-Gore agrees to resign*.

6 p.m. Barry Kent found in sex shop. Charged* with theft* of "grow-it-big" cream and two "ticklers"*.

7 p.m. Coach leaves police station with police escort.

7.30 Police escort waves goodbye.

7.35 Coach driver begs Pandora Braithwaite to keep order.

Dr Laing a famous British psychiatrist (died in 1989) **awestruck** filled with the deepest admiration **heritage** ['herɪtɪdʒ] *G.* Erbe **to dodge** to avoid s.th. by moving away quickly **curator** [ˌkjʊ'reɪtə] s.o. who is in charge of the objects of a museum **cute** *AE* sweet, pretty **to recover** to become better again (after an illness or a shock) **fountain** *G.* Springbrunnen **to predict** *G.* vorhersagen **to head towards** to go into the direction of **mobile** ['məʊbaɪl] **police unit** *G.* mobiles Einsatzkommando **to have a hysterical fit** *G.* einen hysterischen Anfall haben **disgrace** *G.* Schande **profession** a job that needs special training **to resign** to give up a job, to quit **to charge** to say that s.o. has done s.th. criminal **theft** stealing **(French) tickler** *vulgar:* a special kind of condom

7.36 Pandora Braithwaite keeps order.

8 p.m. Ms Fossington-Gore drafts* resignation.

8.30 Coach driver afflicted* by motorway madness.

8.40 Arrive back. Tyres burning. Class Four-D struck dumb* with terror. Ms Fossington-Gore led off by Mr Scruton. Parents up in arms. Coach driver charged by police.

Sunday September 20th

FOURTEENTH AFTER TRINITY. MOON'S LAST QUARTER

Keep having anxiety* attacks every time I think about London, culture or the M1. Pandora's parents are lodging an official complaint* to everyone they can think of.

Monday September 21st

Mr Scruton complimented Pandora and I on our leadership qualities. Ms Fossington-Gore is on sick leave*. All future school trips have been cancelled.

Tuesday September 22nd

The police have dropped charges against coach driver because there is "evidence of severe* provocation". The sex shop are not pressing charges* either because officially Barry Kent is a child. A child! Barry Kent has never been a child.

Wednesday September 23rd

Mr Scruton has now read my report on the trip to London. He gave me two merit marks for it!

It was on the news today that the British Museum is thinking of banning* school parties*.

to draft *G.* entwerfen **to afflict** *here:* to trouble, to affect **to be struck dumb** [dʌm] to be unable to speak because one is angry, shocked, etc. **anxiety** [æŋ'zaɪətɪ] worry, nervousness **to lodge an official complaint** to complain officially **to be on sick leave** *G.* krankgemeldet sein **severe** [sɪ'vɪə] *here:* serious, bad **to press charges** *G.* eine Anzeige aufrechterhalten **to ban** to forbid **party** *here:* group

Thursday September 24th

Pandora and I are enjoying the last of the autumn together by walking through leaves and sniffing* bonfires*. This is the first year I have been able to pass a horse-chestnut* tree without throwing a stick at it.
Pandora says I am maturing* very quickly.

Friday September 25th

Went out conkering* with Nigel tonight. I found five big beauties* and smashed Nigel's into pulp*. Ha! Ha! Ha!

Saturday September 26th

Took Blossom to see Bert. He can't walk far these days.
Blossom is being sold to a rich family, a girl called Camilla is going to learn to ride on her. Pandora says Camilla is so posh* as to be unintelligible*. Bert was dead sad, he said, "You and me will both end up in the knacker's* yard, gel*".

Sunday September 27th
FIFTEENTH AFTER TRINITY

Blossom went off at 10.30 a.m. I gave her a sixteen-pence apple to take her mind off the heartbreak. Pandora ran after the little horse-box shouting, "I've changed my mind", but it carried on.
Pandora has also changed her mind about Ian Smith. She never wants to see another pony or horse again. She is guilt-ridden* about selling Blossom.
Ian Smith turned up at 2.30 p.m. and was turned away. There was an evil* look on his black face as he stood in his horse-box and was driven away. Pandora's father is going to his bank early tomorrow to cancel* the cheque he wrote out last Thursday. There was an evil look on his face as well.

to sniff to smell **bonfire** a big fire, often made to burn rubbish **horse-chestnut** *G.* Rosskastanie **to mature** [məˈtjʊə] to grow up **to conker** to play a children's game with conkers (chestnuts) **beauty** *inf.* s.th. very good **into pulp** *G.* zu Brei **posh** *inf. here:* using a language typical of people of a high social class **unintelligible** [ˌʌnɪnˈtelɪdʒəbl] impossible to understand **knacker** *BE* s.o. who buys and kills worn-out horses for use as animal food **gel** *upper-class pronunciation for:* girl **guilt-ridden** full of guilty feelings **evil** *here inf.* very unpleasant **to cancel** *here: G.* ungültig machen

Monday September 28th
NEW MOON

Bert has got something wrong with his legs. The doctor says he needs daily nursing*. I went in today but he is too heavy for me to lug about*. The district nurse thinks that Bert will be better off in the Alderman Cooper Sunshine Home. But I don't think he will. I pass by it on my way to school. It looks like a museum. The old people look like the exhibits*.

Bert, you are dead old.
Fond of Sabre, beetroot and Woodbines.
We have nothing in common,
I am fourteen and a half,
You are eighty-nine.
You smell, I don't.
Why we are friends
Is a mystery to me.

Tuesday September 29th

Bert doesn't get on with his district nurse. He says he doesn't like having his privates* mauled about* by a woman. Personally, I wouldn't mind it.

Wednesday September 30th

I am glad September is nearly over, it has been nothing but trouble. Blossom gone. Pandora sad. Bert on his last legs. My father still out of work. My mother still besotted with* creep Lucas.

Thursday October 1st

7.30 a.m. Just woke up to find chin covered in spots! How can I face* Pandora?

10 p.m. Avoided Pandora all day but she caught up with me in school dinners. I tried to eat with my hand over my chin but it proved very difficult. I confessed to* her during the yoghurt. She accepted my disability*

to nurse to take care of a sick person **to lug about** *inf.* to carry with difficulty **exhibit** *G.* Ausstellungsstück **privates** genitals **to maul about** to push about, to move **to be besotted with s.o.** *contempt. here:* to like s.o. so much that one seems silly **to face s.o.** *here:* to meet **to confess s.th. to s.o.** *G.* jemandem etwas beichten **disability** being unable, not having the ability

very calmly. She said it made no difference to our love but I couldn't help thinking that her kisses lacked* their usual passion as we were saying goodnight after youth club.

Friday October 2nd

6 p.m. I am very unhappy and have once again turned to great literature for solace*. It's no surprise to me that intellectuals commit suicide*, go mad or die from drink. We feel things more than other people. We know the world is rotten and that chins are ruined by spots. I am reading *Progress, Coexistence and Intellectual Freedom*, by Andrei D. Sakharov*. It is "an inestimably* important document" according to* the cover.

11.30 p.m. Progress, Coexistence and Intellectual Freedom is inestimably *boring*, according to me, Adrian Mole.

I disagree with Sakharov's analysis of the causes of the revivalism* of Stalinism*. We are doing Russia at school so I speak from knowledge.

Saturday October 3rd

Pandora is cooling off. She didn't turn up at Bert's today. I had to do his cleaning on my own.

Went to Sainsbury's as usual in the afternoon; they are selling Christmas cakes. I feel that my life is slipping away.

I am reading *Wuthering Heights**. It is brilliant. If I could get Pandora up somewhere high, I'm sure we could regain our old passion.

Sunday October 4th
SIXTEENTH AFTER TRINITY

Persuaded* Pandora to put her name down for the youth club's mountain survival course in Derbyshire*. Rick Lemon is sending an equipment* list and permission form* to our parents. Or in my case to my parent. I

to lack *here:* to be without **solace** ['sɒləs] comfort (*G.* Trost) **to commit suicide** ['sjʊɪsaɪd] to kill oneself **Sakharov** Russian physicist, Nobel Prize winner (1975) **inestimable** [ɪn'estɪməbl] *G.* unschätzbar **according to** *here:* in the opinion of **revivalism** [rɪ'vaɪvəlɪzəm] *here:* coming back to power **Stalinism** political ideas of Stalin, Russian leader from 1922–1953 **Wuthering Heights** *G.* Sturmhöhen; a novel by Emily Brontë, published in 1847, a story of love and passion in a lonely part of North England **to persuade** [pə'sweɪd] to make people willing to do as one wishes by talking to them **Derbyshire** ['dɑːbɪʃə] a county in North central England **equipment** [ɪ'kwɪpmənt] *G.* Ausrüstung **form** *here: G.* Formular, Vordruck

have only got two weeks to reach peak* condition. I try to do fifty press-ups* a night. I try to do them but fail. Seventeen is my best so far.

Monday October 5th

Bert has been kidnapped by Social Services! They are keeping him at the Alderman Cooper Sunshine Home. I have been to see him. He shares a room with an old man called Thomas Bell. They have both got their names on their ashtrays. Sabre has got a place in the RSPCA hostel.

Our dog has gone missing. It is a portent* of doom*.

Tuesday October 6th
MOON'S FIRST QUARTER

Pandora and I went to visit Bert, but it was a waste of time really.

His room had a strange effect on us, it made us not want to talk about anything. Bert says he is going to sue* Social Services, for depriving him of* his rights. He says he has to go to bed at nine-thirty! It is not fair because he is used to staying up until after *The Epilogue**. We passed the lounge on our way out. The old people sat around the walls in high chairs. The television was on but nobody was watching it, the old people looked as though they were thinking.

Social Services have painted the walls orange to try to cheer the old people up. It doesn't seem to have worked.

Wednesday October 7th

Thomas Bell died in the night. Bert says that nobody leaves the home alive. Bert is the oldest inmate*. He is dead worried about dying. He is now the only man in the entire home. Pandora says that women outlive men. She says it is a sort of bonus* because women have to suffer more earlier on.

Our dog is still missing. I have put an advert in Mr Cherry's shop.

peak *here:* top **press-up** *BE G.* Liegestütz **portent** ['––] *fml.* a warning, a sign **doom** a terrible event in the future **to sue** [sju:] *G.* verklagen **to deprive s.o. of s.th.** to take s.th. away from s.o. **The Epilogue** ['epɪlɒg] *BE* a short (often: religious) programme on TV at the end of the day **inmate** s.o. who lives in a hospital or prison **bonus** ['bəʊnəs] reward, payment

Thursday October 8th

Bert is still alive so I took Sabre to visit him today. We propped* Bert up at the window of his room and he waved to Sabre who was on the lawn outside. Dogs are not allowed inside the home. It is another of their poxy* rules.

Our dog is still missing, now presumed* dead.

Friday October 9th

The matron of the home says that if Bert is dead good he can come out for the day on Sunday. He is coming to our house for Sunday dinner and tea. The phone bill has come. I have hidden it under my mattress. It is for £ 289.19 p.

Saturday October 10th

I am really worried about our dog. It has vanished off the face of* our suburb. Nigel, Pandora and I have walked the cul-de-sacs* looking for it.

Another worry is my father. He lies in bed until noon, then fries a mess in a pan, eats it, opens a can or bottle, then sits and watches *After Noon Plus**. He is making no attempt* to find another job. He needs a bath, a haircut and a shave. It is Parents' Night at school next Tuesday. I have taken his best suit to the cleaner's.

I bought a book from W. H. Smith's*, it was only five pence. It was written by an unsuccessful writer called Drake Fairclough; it is called *Cordon Bleu** *for the Elderly**. Bert is coming tomorrow. Pandora's father has ordered their phone to be taken out. He has found out about the reverse-charge calls.

to prop up *G.* stützen **poxy** *sl. contempt.* very bad, worthless **to presume** to think, to suppose **to vanish off the face of** to disappear completely from **cul-de-sac** ['kʌldəsæk] a street that is closed at one end **After Noon Plus** a TV programme **to make an attempt** to try **W. H. Smith's** name of a British group of bookstores and newsagents **cordon bleu** [ˌkɔːdɔ̃m'blɜː] *French* cooking of a very high standard **elderly** *polite word for:* old

Sunday October 11th
SEVENTEENTH AFTER TRINITY

BERT'S VISIT

I got up early this morning and cleared the furniture out of the hall so that Bert's wheelchair had room for manoeuvre*. I made my father a cup of coffee and took it up to him in bed, then I started cooking geriatric* *coq au vin**. I left it on to boil whilst I went back upstairs to reawaken my father. When I got downstairs I knew that I'd made a mess* of the *coq au vin*. All the vinegar* had boiled away and left burnt chicken. I was most disappointed because I was thinking of making my debut as a cook today. I wanted to impress Pandora with my multi talents, I think she is getting a bit bored with my conversation about great literature and the Norwegian leather industry.

Bert insisted on* bringing a big trunk* with him when Pandora's father picked him up at the home. So what with that and his wheelchair and Bert sprawling* all over the back seat I was forced to crouch* in the hatch of the hatchback car*. It took ages to get Bert out of the car and into his wheelchair. Almost as long as it took me to get my father out of bed.

Pandora's father stayed for a quick drink, then a pre-lunch one, then a chaser*, then one for the road. Then he had one to prove that he never got drunk during the day. Pandora's lips started to go thin (women must teach young girls to do this). Then she confiscated her father's car keys and phoned her mother to come and collect the car. I had to endure watching my father do his imitation of some bloke called Frank Sinatra singing "One for my baby and one more for the road". Pandora's father pretended to be the bartender with our Tupperware* custard jug. They were both drunkenly singing when Pandora's mother came in. Her lips were so thin they had practically disappeared. She ordered Pandora and Pandora's father out into the car, then she said that it was about time my father pulled himself together. She said she knew my father felt humiliated*, alienated* and bitter because he was unemployed, but that he was

manoeuvre [mə'nuːvə] *here:* moving about **geriatric** [ˌdʒerɪ'ætrɪk] *here:* good for old people **coq au vin** [kɔk o'vɛ̃] *French* a chicken with red wine, onions, etc. **to make a mess of s.th.** to ruin s.th. **vinegar** *G.* Essig **to insist on** to say firmly, to demand strongly **trunk** a large box for travelling **to sprawl** to sit down and spread one's arms and legs **to crouch** *G.* sich zusammenkauern **hatchback car** a car with an extra door at the back which opens upwards **chaser** *here:* a milder drink after a strong one **Tupperware** (trademark) made of plastic **humiliated** [hjuː'mɪlɪeɪtɪd] *G.* gedemütigt **alienated** ['eɪljəneɪtɪd] *here:* angry

setting a bad example to an impressionable* adolescent*. Then she drove off at 10 mph*. Pandora blew me a kiss through the rear windscreen.

I object* strongly! Nothing my father does impresses me any more. Had Vesta curry and rice for dinner, during which Mrs Singh came round and talked Hindi to Bert. She seemed to find our curry very funny, she kept pointing to it and laughing. Sometimes I think I am the only person in the world who still has manners*.

Bert told my father that he is convinced* the matron is trying to poison* him (Bert, not my father), but my father said that all institutional* food is the same. When it was time to go home, Bert started crying. He said, "Don't make me go back there", and other sad things. My father explained that we didn't have the skill to look after him at our house, so Bert was wheeled to the car (although he kept putting the brake of the wheelchair on). He asked us to keep his trunk at our house. He said it was to be opened on his death. The key is round his neck on a bit of string.

Dog is still AWOL*.

Monday October 12th

COLUMBUS DAY*, USA. THANKSGIVING DAY, CANADA

Went to the "off-the-streets" youth club tonight. Rick Lemon gave us a lecture* on survival* techniques. He said that the best thing to do if you are suffering from hypothermia* is to climb into a plastic bag with a naked woman. Pandora made a formal objection, and Rick Lemon's girlfriend, Tit, got up and walked away. It is just my luck to be on the mountain with a frigid* woman!

RIP* Dog.

impressionable not critical, believing s.th. easily **adolescent** [ˌædəʊˈlesnt] a young person between 13–16 years old **mph** *short for:* miles per hour **to object** [–ˈ–] to say that one is against s.th. **manners** ways of behaving well **to be convinced** to believe strongly **to poison** *G.* vergiften **institutional** [ˌɪnstɪˈtjuːʃənl] *here:* found in homes, hospitals, etc. **AWOL** *a military expression* absent without leave (permission) **Columbus Day** a US holiday celebrating the discovery of America (1492) **to give a lecture on** *here:* to talk about s.th. in detail **survival** [səˈvaɪvl] *G.* Überleben **hypothermia** [ˌhaɪpəʊˈθɜːmɪə] illness because one's body temperature is too low **frigid** [ˈfrɪdʒɪd] cold, not liking sex **RIP** *Latin* Requiescat in pace! (May he/she rest in peace!)

Tuesday October 13th

FULL MOON

Had an angry phone call from my grandma to ask when we were coming round to collect the dog! The stupid dog turned up at her house on the 6th October. I went round immediately and was shocked at the dog's condition: it looks old and grey. In human years it is eleven years old. In dog years it should be drawing a pension. I have never seen a dog age so quickly. Those eight days with grandma must have been hell. My grandma is very strict.

Wednesday October 14th

I have nearly got used to the old ladies in the home now. I call in every afternoon on my way home from school. They seem pleased to see me. One of them is knitting me a balaclava* for my survival weekend. She is called Queenie.

Did thirty-six and a half press-ups tonight.

Thursday October 15th

Went to the youth club to try yukky, lousy old walking boots for size. Rick Lemon has hired them from a mountaineering shop. To make mine fit I have to wear three pairs of socks. Six of us are going. Rick is leading us.

He is unqualified but experienced in surviving bad conditions. He was born and brought up in Kirby New Town. I went to Sainsbury's and bought my survival food. We have got to carry our food and equipment in our rucksacks, so weight is an important factor. I bought:

1 box cornflakes	1 lb cheese
2 pints milk	2 packets biscuits
box tea-bags	2 lb sugar
tin rhubarb	toilet roll
5 lb* spuds*	washing-up liquid
1/2 lb lard*	2 tins tuna
1/2 lb butter	1 tin stewed steak
2 loaves bread	1 tin carrots

balaclava [ˌbæləˈklɑːvə] a woollen covering which covers every part of the head except the face **lb** *Latin* libra = a pound **spud** *inf.* potato **lard** *G.* Schweineschmalz

I could hardly carry my survival food home from Sainsbury's, so how I will manage it on a march across the hills I don't know! My father suggested leaving something out. So I have not packed the toilet roll or cornflakes.

Friday October 16th

Have decided not to take my diary to Derbyshire. I cannot guarantee that it will not be read by hostile* eyes. Besides it won't fit into my rucksack.

Must finish now, the mini-bus is outside papping* its hooter*.

Saturday October 17th

Sunday October 18th

EIGHTEENTH AFTER TRINITY

8 p.m. It is wonderful to be back in civilization!

I have lived like an ignoble* savage* for the past two days! Sleeping on rough ground with only a sleeping-bag between me and the elements! Trying to cook chips over a tiny primus stove! Trudging* through streams in my torturous* boots! Having to perform my natural functions* out in the open! Wiping my bum on leaves! Not being able to have a bath or clean my teeth! No televison or radio or anything! Rick Lemon wouldn't even let us sit in the mini-bus when it started to rain! He said we ought to make a shelter* out of nature's bounty*! Pandora found a plastic animal–food sack so we took it in turns sitting under it.

How I survived I don't know. My eggs broke, my bread got saturated*, my biscuits got crushed and nobody had a tinopener. I nearly starved. Thank God cheese doesn't leak*, break, soak up water or come in a tin. I was glad when we were found and taken to the Mountain Rescue* headquarters. Rick Lemon was told off for not having a map or compass. Rick said he knew the hills like the back of his hand. The chief mountain rescuer said that Rick must have been wearing gloves because

hostile ['hɒstaɪl] extremely unfriendly **to pap** *inf. here:* to sound **hooter** a car horn or siren **ignoble** not honourable, morally unacceptable **savage** ['sævɪdʒ] *here:* a wild person, living away from civilization **to trudge** to walk with tired steps **torturous** ['tɔːtʃərəz] making suffer, causing pain **to perform one's natural functions** *cf. G.* sein Geschäft verrichten **shelter** *here:* protection against bad weather **bounty** *G.* reiche Fülle **to saturate** ['sætʃəreɪt] to make completely wet **to leak** *G.* auslaufen, undicht sein **Mountain Rescue** ['reskjuː] *G.* Bergwacht

we were seven miles from our mini-bus and heading* in the wrong direction!

I shall now sleep in a bed for the first time in two days. No school tomorrow because of blisters*.

Monday October 19th

I have got to rest my feet for two days. Doctor Gray was very unpleasant: he said that he resented* being called out for a few foot blisters.

I was very surprised at his attitude. It is a well-known fact that mountaineers get gangrene* of the toes.

Tuesday October 20th
MOON'S LAST QUARTER

Here I am lying in bed unable to walk because of excruciating* pain and my father carries out his parental responsibilities* by throwing a few bacon sandwiches at me three times a day!

If my mother doesn't come home soon I will end up deprived* and maladjusted*. I am already neglected*.

Wednesday October 21st

Hobbled* to school. All the teachers were wearing their best clothes because it is Parents' Evening tonight. My father got cleaned up and put his best suit on. He looked OK, Thank God! Nobody could tell he was unemployed. My teachers all told him that I was a credit to* the school.

Barry Kent's father was looking as sick as a pig. Ha! Ha! Ha!

Thursday October 22nd

Limped* half-way to school. Dog followed me. Limped back home. Shut dog in coal shed. Limped all the way to school. Fifteen minutes late. Mr Scruton said it was not setting a good example for the late prefect to be

to head *here:* to walk **blister** *G.* Blase **to resent** [rɪ'zent] to feel angry about **gangrene** ['gæŋgriːn] *G.* Wundbrand **excruciating** [ɪk'skruːʃɪeɪtɪŋ] *here:* extremely bad **responsibility** *G.* Verantwortung **deprived** without money, food, education, etc. **maladjusted** [ˌmælə'dʒʌstɪd] not having a good relationship with other people **to neglect** not to take care of **to hobble** *G.* humpeln, hinken **to be a credit to s.th. or s.o.** *G.* jemandem Ehre machen **to limp** *G.* hinken

late. It is all right for him to talk! He can ride to school in a Ford Cortina and then all he has to do is be in charge of a school. I have got a lot of problems and no car.

Friday October 23rd

I have had a letter from the hospital to say that I have got to have my tonsils* out on Tuesday the twenty-seventh. This has come as a complete shock to me! My father says I have been on the waiting list since I was five years old! So I have had to endure an annual* bout* of tonsillitis for nine years just because the National Health Service* is starved* of finance!

Why can't midwives* remove* babies' tonsils at birth? It would save a lot of trouble, pain and money.

Saturday October 24th
UNITED NATIONS' DAY

Went shopping for new dressing gown, slippers, pyjamas, and toiletries. My father was moaning as usual. He said he didn't see why I couldn't just wear my old night-clothes in hospital. I told him that I would look ridiculous in my Peter Pan* dressing gown and Winnie the Pooh* pyjamas. Apart from the yukky design they are too small and covered in patches*. He said that when he was a lad* he slept in a nightshirt made out of two coal sacks stitched together. I phoned my grandma to check this suspicious statement and my father was forced to repeat it down the phone. My grandma said that they were not coal sacks but flour sacks, so I now know that my father is a pathological* liar!

My hospital rig* came to fifty-four pounds nineteen; this is before fruit, chocolates and Lucozade. Pandora said I looked like Noël Coward* in my new bri-nylon dressing gown. I said, "Thanks, Pandora", although to be honest I don't know who Noël Coward is or was. I hope he's not a mass murderer or anything.

tonsils *G.* Mandeln **annual** [ˈænjʊəl] yearly, every year **bout** [baʊt] a short period **National Health Service** public medical service in Britain, paid for by people's taxes (*G.* Steuern) and therefore free to every patient **to be starved of** to be without **midwife** *G.* Hebamme **to remove** to take away **Peter Pan** boy hero of a play by J. M. Barrie (1904) **Winnie the Pooh** a toy bear in two popular children's books by A. A. Milne (1882–1956) **patch** *here: G.* Flicken **lad** boy, young man **pathological** [ˌpæθəˈlɒdʒɪkl] *here: G.* krankhaft, zwanghaft **rig** equipment (*G.* Ausrüstung) **Noël Coward** (1899–1973) a British actor and writer of comedies

Sunday October 25th

NINETEENTH AFTER TRINITY. BRITISH SUMMER TIME ENDS

Phoned my mother to tell her about my coming surgical* ordeal*. No reply*. This is typical. She would sooner be out having fun with creep Lucas than comforting her only child!

Grandma rang and said that she knew somebody who knew somebody who knew somebody who had their tonsils out and bled* to death on the operating theatre* table. She ended up by saying, "Don't worry Adrian, I'm sure everything will be all right for you".

Thanks a million, grandma!

Monday October 26th

BANK HOLIDAY IN THE REP. OF IRELAND

11 a.m. I did my packing, then went to see Bert. He is sinking* fast so it could be the last time we see each other. Bert also knows somebody who bled to death after a tonsils' extraction*. I hope it's the same person.

Said goodbye to Pandora: she wept very touchingly. She brought me one of Blossom's old horseshoes to take into hospital. She said a friend of her father had a cyst* removed and didn't come out of the anaesthetic*. I'm being admitted to Ivy Swallow Ward at 2 p.m. Greenwich Mean Time*.

6 p.m. My father has just left my bedside after four hours of waiting around for permission to leave. I have had every part of my body examined. Liquid* substances have been taken from me, I have been weighed and bathed, measured and prodded* and poked*, but nobody has looked in my throat!

I have put our family medical dictionary on my bedside table so that the doctors see it and are impressed. I can't tell what the rest of the ward is like yet because the nurses have forgotten to remove the screens*. A notice has been hung over my bed; it says "Liquids Only". I am dead scared.

surgical ['sɜːdʒɪkl] *G.* operativ, chirurgisch **ordeal** [ɔː'diːl] extremely unpleasant situation **reply** answer **to bleed, bled, bled** to lose blood **operating theatre** the room in a hospital where doctors operate on patients **to sink** *here:* to become weaker and weaker **extraction** *here:* taking out **cyst** [sɪst] *G.* Geschwulst **anaesthetic** [ˌænɪs'θetɪk] *G.* Betäubung **Greenwich Mean Time** (GMT) the standard time for Britain **liquid** *G.* flüssig **to prod/to poke** to push quickly with one's finger **screen** *G.* Wandschirm, Trennwand

10 p.m. I am starving! A black nurse has taken all my food and drink away. I am supposed to go to sleep but it is like bedlam* in here. Old men keep falling out of bed.

Midnight. There is a new notice over my bed; it says "Nil* by Mouth". I am dying of thirst! I would give my right arm for a can of Low Cal*.

Tuesday October 27th
NEW MOON

4 a.m. I am dehydrated*!

6 a.m. Just been woken up! Operation is not until 10 a.m. So why couldn't they let me sleep? I have got to have another bath. I told them that it is the *inside* of my body that is being operated on, but they don't listen.

7 a.m. A Chinese nurse stayed in the bathroom to make sure I didn't drink any water. She kept staring so I had to put a hospital sponge over my thing.

7.30 a.m. I am dressed like a lunatic, ready for the operation. I have had an injection, it is supposed to make you sleepy but I'm wide awake listening to a row about a patient's lost notes.

8 a.m. My mouth is completely dry, I shall go mad from thirst, I haven't had a drink since nine forty-five last night. I feel very floaty*, the cracks in the ceiling are very interesting. I have got to find somewhere to hide my diary. I don't want prying* Nosy Parkers* reading it.

8.30 a.m. My mother is at my bedside! She is going to put my diary in her organizer-handbag. She has promised (on the dog's life) not to read it.

8.45 a.m. My mother is in the hospital grounds smoking a cigarette. She is looking old and haggard*. All the debauchery* is catching up with her.

9 a.m. The operating trolley keeps coming into the ward and dumping unconscious* men into beds. The trolley-pushers are wearing green overalls and wellingtons*. There must be loads of blood on the floor of the theatre!

bedlam ['bedləm] *here:* chaos **nil** *Latin* nothing **Low Cal** (trademark) a low calorie drink **to dehydrate** [ˌdiːˈhaɪdreɪt] *here:* to make a person lose a lot of water **floaty** *G.* schwebend **to pry** [praɪ] to be very curious **Nosy Parker** *BE inf. contempt.* s.o. who is too interested in other people's affairs **haggard** looking tired and unhappy **debauchery** [dɪˈbɔːtʃərɪ] immoral behaviour **unconscious** [ʌnˈkɒnʃəs] *G.* ohnmächtig **wellingtons** *BE* waterproof rubber boots

9.15 a.m. The trolley is coming in my direction!

Midnight. I am devoid of* tonsils. I am in a torrent* of pain. It took my mother thirteen minutes to find my diary. She doesn't know her way round her organizer-handbag yet. It has got seventeen compartments*.

Wednesday October 28th

I am unable to speak. Even groaning* causes agony*.

Thursday October 29th

I have been moved to a side ward. My suffering is too much for the other patients to bear.

Had a "get well" card from Bert and Sabre.

Friday October 30th

I was able to sip a little of grandma's broth* today. She brought it in her Thermos flask. My father brought me a family pack of crisps; he might just as well have brought me razor blades!

Pandora came at visiting time, I had little to whisper to her. Conversation palls* when one is hovering* between life and death.

Saturday October 31st
HALLOWE'EN*

3 a.m. I have been forced to complain about the noise coming from the nurses' home. I am sick of listening (and watching) drunken nurses and off-duty policemen cavorting around* the grounds dressed as witches* and wizards*. Nurse Boldry was doing something particularly unpleasant with a pumpkin*.

I am joining BUPA* as soon as they'll have me.

devoid of without, free from **torrent** a violent stream **compartment** *here:* *G.* Fach **to groan** *G.* stöhnen **agony** ['ægənɪ] extreme pain **broth** *G.* Fleischbrühe **to pall** [pɔːl] to become uninteresting **to hover** *here:* *G.* schweben **Hallowe'en** [ˌhæləʊ'iːn] a day of costumes and fancy dress parties **to cavort around** to jump around noisily **witch** *G.* Hexe **wizard** *G.* Zauberer, Hexenmeister **pumpkin** *G.* Kürbis **BUPA** an insurance company that pays for private medical care

Sunday November 1st
TWENTIETH AFTER TRINITY

The nurses have been very cold towards me. They say that I am taking up a bed that could be used by an ill person! I have got to eat a bowl of cornflakes before they let me out. So far I have refused; I cannot bear the pain.

Monday November 2nd

Nurse Boldry forced a spoon of cornflakes down my damaged throat, then, before I could digest* it, she started stripping* my bed. She offered to pay for a taxi, but I told her that I would wait for my father to come and carry me out to the car.

Tuesday November 3rd
ELECTION DAY*, USA

I am in my own bed. Pandora is a tower of strength*. She and I communicate without words. My voice has been damaged by the operation.

Wednesday November 4th

Today I croaked my first words for a week. I said, "Dad, phone mum and tell her that I am over the worst". My father was overcome with relief* and emotion. His laughter was close to hysteria.

Thursday November 5th
MOON'S FIRST QUARTER

Dr Gray says my malfunctioning* voice is "only adolescent wobble*". He is always in a bad mood!

He expected me to stagger to his surgery and queue in a germ*-filled waiting room! He said I ought to be outside with other lads of my age building a bonfire*. I told him that I was too old for such paganistic* rituals. He said he was forty-seven and he still enjoyed a good burn-up.

Forty-seven! It explains a lot, he should be pensioned off.

to digest *G.* verdauen **to strip** *here:* to take the blankets away **Election Day** day for state elections (*G.* Wahlen) in the USA **a tower of strength** *G.* Stütze, großer Rückhalt **relief** *G.* Erleichterung **malfunctioning** [ˌmælˈfʌŋkʃnɪŋ] not working properly **wobble** a voice that is weak and sometimes high, sometimes low **germ** *G.* Bazille **bonfire** a big fire, made to celebrate s. th. **paganistic** [ˌpeɪgənˈɪstɪk] *contempt. here:* not Christian

Friday November 6th

My father is taking me to an organized bonfire party tomorrow (providing I am up to* it, of course). It is being held to raise funds* for Marriage Guidance Councillors'* expenses*.

Pandora's mother is cooking the food and Pandora's father is in charge of the fireworks. My father is going to be in charge of lighting the bonfire so I'm going to stand at least a hundred metres away. I have seen him singe* his eyebrows many times.

Last night some irresponsible* people down our street had bonfire parties in their own back gardens!

Yes!

In spite of* being warned of all the dangers by the radio, television, *Blue Peter** and the media* they went selfishly* ahead. There were no accidents, but surely this was only luck.

Saturday November 7th

The Marriage Guidance Council bonfire was massive. It was a good community effort. Mr Cherry donated* hundreds of copies of a magazine called *Now*! He said they had been cluttering* up the back room of his shop for over a year.

Pandora burnt her collection of *Jackie* comics, she said that they "don't bear* feminist* analysis" and she "wouldn't like them to get into young girls' hands".

Mr Singh and all the little Singhs brought along Indian firecrackers. They are much louder than English ones. I was glad our dog was locked in the coal shed with cotton wool in its ears.

Nobody was seriously burnt, but I think it was a mistake to hand out fireworks at the same time the food was being served.

I burnt the red phone bill that came this morning.

to be up to s.th. *here:* to be strong enough for s.th. **to raise funds** to collect/get money **Marriage Guidance Councillor** *G.* Eheberater **expenses** the money one spends while doing a job **to singe** [sɪndʒ] *G.* (ver)sengen **irresponsible** *G.* unverantwortlich **in spite of** *G.* trotz **Blue Peter** a popular children's programme on British TV **(mass)media** *plural* TV, radio and newspapers **selfish** egoistic **to donate** [dəʊ'neɪt] to give without wanting money for it **to clutter up** to make untidy by filling with useless things **to bear** *here: G.* standhalten **feminist** believing that women should have the same rights and job opportunities as men

Sunday November 8th

TWENTY-FIRST AFTER TRINITY. REMEMBRANCE SUNDAY

Our street is full of acrid* smoke. I went to see the bonfire, the *Now* magazines are still in the hot ashes, they are refusing to burn properly. (Our red phone bill has disappeared, thank God!)

Mr Cherry is going to have to dig a big pit* and pour quicklime* over the *Now* magazines before they choke* the whole suburb.

Went to see Bert. He was out with Queenie.

Monday November 9th

Back to school. The dog is at the vet's having the cotton wool surgically removed.

Tuesday November 10th

My nippels* have swollen! I am turning into a girl!!!

Wednesday November 11th

VETERANS' DAY, USA. REMEMBRANCE DAY*, CANADA. FULL MOON

Dr Gray has struck me off his list! He said nipple-swelling is common in boys. Usually they get it when they are twelve and a half. Dr Gray said I was emotionally and physically immature*! How can I be immature? I have had a rejection* letter from the BBC! And how could I have walked to the surgery* with swollen nipples?

I don't know why he calls it a surgery anyway; he never does any surgery in it.

Thursday November 12th

Told Mr Jones I couldn't do PE because of swollen nipples. He was extremely crude* in his attitude. I don't know what they teach them at teacher-training college.

acrid ['ækrɪd] strong, sharp **pit** a large hole in the ground **quicklime** *G.* Kalk **to choke** to stop from breathing **nipple** *G.* Brustwarze **Remembrance Day** a day celebrating the 11th November 1918, the final day of the First World War **immature** [ˌɪmə'tjʊə] *here:* childish **rejection** [rɪ'dʒekʃn] *here: G.* Ablehnung **surgery** ['sɜːdʒərɪ] *G.* 1. Praxis 2. Chirurgie **crude** [kruːd] vulgar, rude

Friday November 13th

Pandora and I had a frank talk about our relationship tonight. She doesn't want to marry me in two years' time!

She wants to have a career instead!

Naturally I am devastated* by this blow*. I told her I wouldn't mind her having a little job in a cake shop or something after our wedding, but she said she intended* to go to university and that the only time she would enter a cake shop would be to buy a large crusty*.

Harsh words were exchanged between us. (Hers were harsher than mine.)

Saturday November 14th

Charred* *Now*! magazines are blowing all over our cul-de-sac. They seem to have special powers of survival. The council have sent a special cleaning squad* to try and trap them all.

The dog's ears are now clear of cotton wool. It only pretends not to hear.

Went to see B.B. but he is out with Queenie. She is pushing him around the leisure centre.

Sunday November 15th
TWENTY-SECOND AFTER TRINITY

Read *A Town Like Alice**, by Nevil Shute*, it is dead brill*. I wish I had an intellectual friend whom I could discuss great literature with. My father thinks *A Town Like Alice* was written by Lewis Carroll*.

Monday November 16th

I came home from school with a headache. All the noise and shouting and bullying* is getting me down! Surely teachers should be better behaved!

to devastate ['devəsteɪt] to destroy completely **blow** disappointment **to intend** to plan **crusty** (bread) *G.* knusprig **to char** [tʃɑː] to become black by burning **squad** *here:* a group of people working as a team **A Town Like Alice** a novel by **Nevil Shute**, published in 1950 **brill.** *inf.* brilliant **Lewis Caroll** writer of *Alice in Wonderland* (1865) **to bully** ['bʊlɪ] to frighten or hurt a weaker person

Tuesday November 17th

My father is a serious worry to me. Even the continuing news of Princess Diana's conception* does not cheer him up.

Grandma has already knitted three pairs of bootees* and sent them off care of Buckingham Palace. She is a true patriot.

Wednesday November 18th

MOON'S LAST QUARTER

The trees are stark naked.
Their autumnal clothes
Litter the pavements.
Council sweepers apply fire
Thus creating municipal* pyres*.
I, Adrian Mole,
Kick them
And burn my Hush Puppies.

I have copied it out carefully and sent it to John Tydeman at the BBC. He strikes me as a man who might like poems about autumn leaves.

I have got to get something broadcast or printed soon else Pandora will lose all respect for me.

Thursday November 19th

Pandora has suggested I start a literary magazine using the school duplicator. I wrote the first edition during dinner-time. It is called *The Voice of Youth*.

Friday November 20th

Pandora looked at *the Voice of Youth*. She suggested that instead of writing the whole magazine myself, I invite contributions* from other talented scribblers*.

She said she would do a piece about window-box gardening. Claire Neilson has submitted* a punk poem, it is very avant garde*, but I am not afraid to break new ground*.

conception [kən'sepʃn] *here:* *G.* Schwangerschaft (pregnancy) **bootee** ['bu:tɪ:] a baby's woollen boot **municipal** [mju:'nɪsɪpl] belonging to a town or city **pyre** ['paɪə] *G.* Scheiterhaufen **contribution** [ˌkɒntrɪ'bju:ʃn] *G.* Beitrag **scribbler** *inf.* a writer **to submit** *here:* to give **avant garde** [ˌævɑ̃:ŋ 'gɑ:d] *French* very modern, progressive **to break new ground** to introduce or do s.th. new

Punk Poem
Society is puke*,
Soiled* vomit*.
On the Union Jack
Sid was vicious*
Johnnie's rotten,
Dead, dead, dead.
Killed by greyness.
England stinks.
Sewer* of the world.
Cess-pit* of Europe.
Hail* punks,
Kings and Queens
Of the street.

She wants it put in under an assumed name, her father is a Conservative councillor*.

Nigel has written a short piece about racing-bike maintenance*. It is very boring but I can't tell him because he is my best friend.

We go to press on Wednesday.

Pandora is typing the stencils* over the weekend.

Here is my first editorial:*

Hi Kids,

Well here's your very own school magazine. Yes! Written and produced entirely using child labour. I have tried to break new ground in our first edition. Many of you will be unaware of* the miracles of window-box gardening and the joys of racing-bike maintenance. If so, hang on to your hats, you're in for a magic surprise!

ADRIAN MOLE, EDITOR

We are going to charge twenty-five pence a copy.

puke *sl.*/**vomit** food brought back from the stomach through the mouth **to soil** to make dirty **vicious** ['vɪʃəs] violent, dangerous, evil **sewer** [sjʊə] *G.* Kloake **cess-pit** *G.* Jauchegrube **hail** *arch.* welcome! **councillor** *here: G.* Stadtrat **maintenance** ['meɪntənəns] keeping s.th. in a good condition **stencil** *G.* Matritze **editorial** [ˌedɪ'tɔːrɪəl] *G.* Leitartikel **unaware of** not knowing, ignorant of

Saturday November 21st

Pandora's father has stolen a box of stencils from his office. As I write, Pandora is typing the first pages of *The Voice of Youth*. I am half-way through writing an exposé* about Barry Kent. It is called "Barry Kent: The Truth!" He hasn't dared to lay a finger on me since grandma's dramatic intervention, so I know I shall be safe.

Too busy to go and see Bert, I will go tomorrow.

Sunday November 22nd
LAST AFTER TRINITY

Finished the exposé on Barry Kent. It will rock* the school to its foundations*. I have mentioned Barry Kent's sexual perversions—all about his disgusting practice of showing his thing for five pence a look.

Monday November 23rd

Had a Christmas card from grandma, and a letter from the post office to say that they are cutting the phone off!

Forgot to call round and see Bert. Pandora and I were too busy putting the paper to bed*. How I wish I was putting Pandora to bed.

2 a.m. What am I going to do about the phone bill?

Tuesday November 24th

Nigel has just gone off in a sulk. He objected to the editing* I did on his article. I tried to point out to him that one thousand five hundred words on bicycle spokes was pure self-indulgence*, but he wouldn't listen. He has withdrawn* his article. Thank God! Two pages less to fold.

The Voice of Youth hits the classrooms tomorrow.

Must go and see Bert tomorrow.

Wednesday November 25th

We have been hit by a wildcat strike*! Mrs Claricoates, the school secretary, has refused to handle *The Voice of Youth*. She says there is nothing

exposé [eks'pəʊzeɪ] a short statement about a number of facts **to rock** to move, to swing from side to side **foundation** the parts of a building which are below ground and which are built first **to put a paper to bed** (journalism) to make a newspaper ready for publication **to edit** *here:* to correct, to make fit for publication **self-indulgence** [ˌselfɪn'dʌldʒəns] *here: G.* Maßlosigkeit **to withdraw** *here:* to take back **wildcat strike** a sudden unofficial strike

in her job description to say she has to mess about with school magazines.

The editorial team offered to duplicate copies ourselves, but Mrs Claricoates says that she alone knows how to "work the wretched* thing". I am in despair. A whole six hours' work wasted!

Thursday November 26th

THANKSGIVING DAY, USA. NEW MOON

Pandora's father is photocopying *The Voice of Youth* on his office machine. He didn't want to, but Pandora sulked in her room and refused to eat until he agreed.

Friday November 27th

Five hundred copies of *The Voice of Youth* were on sale in the dinner hall today.

Five hundred copies were locked in the games cupboard by the end of the afternoon. Not one copy was sold! Not one! My fellow pupils are nothing but Philistines* and Morons*!

We are dropping the price to twenty pence on Monday.

My mother phoned and wanted to speak to my father. I told her that he is on a fishing weekend with the Society of Redundant Electric Storage Heater Salesmen.

A postcard from the post office to say that unless my father phones the post office before five-thirty our phone will be disconnected*.

Saturday November 28th

A telegram! Adressed to me! The BBC? No, from my mother:

ADRIAN STOP COMING HOME STOP

What does she mean "Stop coming home"? How can I "stop coming home"? I live here.

The phone has been cut off! I am considering* running away from home.

wretched ['retʃɪd] *inf.* of bad quality **Philistine** ['fɪlɪstaɪn] *contempt.* a person who does not like literature and is even proud of this **moron** *inf. contempt.* idiot **to disconnect** to cut off **to consider** to think about

Sunday November 29th
ADVENT SUNDAY

My mother has just turned up with no warning! She had all her suitcases with her. She has thrown herself on the mercy* of my father. My father has just thrown himself on the body of my mother. I tactfully withdrew* to my bedroom where I am now trying to work out how I feel about my mother's return. On the whole I am over the moon*, but I'm dreading* her looking around our squalid house. She will go mad when she finds out that I have lent Pandora her fox-fur* coat.

Monday November 30th
ST ANDREW'S* DAY

My mother and father were still in bed when I left for school.

Sold one copy of *The Voice of Youth*, to Barry Kent. He wanted to discover the truth about himself. He is a slow reader so it will probably take him until Friday to find out. We are going to try dropping the price to fifteen pence to try to stimulate* demand*. There are now four hundred and ninety-nine copies to be sold!

My mother and father are in bed again and it's only 9 p.m.!

The dog is very pleased my mother is back. It has been going about smiling all day.

Tuesday December 1st

I called the post office and pretended to be my father. I spoke in a very deep voice and told a lot of lies. I said that I, George Mole, had been in a lunatic asylum* for three months and I needed the phone to ring up the Samaritans, etc. The woman sounded dead horrible, she said she was fed up with hearing lame excuses from irresponsible* non-payers. She said that the phone would only be reconnected* when £ 289.19 had been paid, plus £ 40 reconnection fee, plus a deposit* of £ 40.

Three hundred and sixty-nine pounds! When my parents get out of bed and discover the lack of dialling tone*, I will be done for!

mercy willingness to forgive s.o. **to withdraw** *here:* to go away **over the moon** *inf.* very happy **to dread** [dred] to fear very much **fox-fur** *G.* Fuchspelz **St Andrew** the patron saint of Scotland **to stimulate** to cause to be more active **demand** *here: G.* Nachfrage **lunatic asylum** ['lu:nətɪk ə'saɪləm] *old use* a home for mad people **irresponsible** [ˌɪrɪ'spɒnsəbl] *G.* unverantwortlich **to reconnect** *here: G.* wieder anschließen **deposit** [–'––] *here: G.* Kaution **dialling tone** *G.* Freizeichen

Wednesday December 2nd

My father tried to phone up after a job today! He has gone beserk.

My mother cleaned my bedroom, she turned up my mattress and found the *Big and Bouncys* and the blue phone bill.

I sat on the kitchen stool while they interrogated* me and shouted abuse*. My father wanted to give me a "to-within-an-inch-of-his-life trashing*", but my mother stopped him. She said, "It would be more of a punishment to make the tight-fisted* sod* cough up* some of his building-society savings". So that is what I'm being forced to do.

Now I will never be an owner-occupier*.

Thursday December 3rd

Drew out two hundred pounds from my building-society account. I don't mind admitting that there were tears in my eyes. It will take another fourteen years before I can replace it.

Friday December 4th
MOON'S FIRST QUARTER

I am suffering from severe depression. It is all Pandora's father's fault. He should have had a holiday in England.

Saturday December 5th

Had a letter from grandma to ask why I hadn't sent her a Christmas card yet.

Sunday December 6th
SECOND IN ADVENT

I am still being treated* like a criminal. My mother and father are not speaking to me, and I'm not allowed out. I might just as well turn to delinquency*.

to interrogate [ɪn'terəʊgeɪt] to ask (police-like) questions **abuse** unfriendly, rude words **to thrash to within an inch of one's life** *inf.* to hit very hard **tight-fisted** *inf.* unwilling to spend money **sod** *swear word* an unpleasant person **to cough up money** *inf.* to give money **owner occupier** s.o. who lives in a house which belongs to him/her **to treat** *G.* behandeln **delinquency** [dɪ'lɪŋkwənsɪ] being a criminal

Monday December 7th

Stole a Kevin Keegan key ring from Mr Cherry's shop. It will do for Nigel's Christmas present.

Tuesday December 8th

I am dead worried about the key ring; we did Morals and Ethics at school today.

Wednesday December 9th

Can't sleep for worrying about the key ring. The papers are full of stories about old ladies getting done* for shoplifting. I tried to overpay Mr Cherry for my Mars bar, but he called me back and gave me my change.

Thursday December 10th

Had a dream about a jailer locking me in a prison cell. The big iron key was attached* to the Kevin Keegan key ring.

The lousy, stinking, sodding* phone is reconnected!

Friday December 11th FULL MOON

Phoned the Samaritans and confessed* my crime. The man said, "Put it back then, lad". I will do it tomorrow.

Saturday December 12th

Mr Cherry caught me in the act of replacing* the key ring. He has written a letter to my parents. I might as well do myself in*.

Sunday December 13th THIRD IN ADVENT

Thank God there is no post on Sundays.

My mother and father had a festive time decorating the Christmas tree. I watched them hanging the baubles* with a heavy heart.

I am reading *Crime and Punishment**. It is the most true book I have ever read.

to get done *inf.* to get arrested **to attach** *G.* festmachen **sodding** *swear word* (used by angry people) **to confess** *here:* to admit **to replace** to put back **to do s.o. in** *inf.* to kill s.o. **baubles** *here: G.* Weihnachtsschmuck **Crime and Punishment** a novel by the Russian writer Dostoevsky (1866)

Monday December 14th

Got up at 5 a.m. to intercept* the postman. Took the dog for a walk in the drizzle. (It wanted to stay asleep, but I wouldn't let it.) The dog moaned and complained all the way round the block so in the end I let it climb back into its cardboard box. I wish I was a dog; they haven't got any ethics or morals.

The postman delivered the letters at seven-thirty when I was sitting on the toilet. This is just my luck!

My father collected the letters and put them behind the clock. I had a quick look through them while he was coughing on his first cigarette of the day. Sure enough there was one addressed to my parents in Mr Cherry's uneducated handwriting!

My mother and father slopped over each other for a few minutes and then opened the letters whilst their Rice Krispies were going soggy*. There were seven lousy Christmas cards, which they put up on a string over the fireplace. My eyes were focused on* Mr Cherry's letter. My mother opened it, read it and said, "George, that old git Cherry's sent his bloody paper bill in". Then they ate their Rice Krispies and that was that. I wasted a lot of adrenalin worrying. I won't have enough left if I'm not careful.

Tuesday December 15th

My mother has told me why she left creep Lucas and returned to my father. She said, "Bimbo treated me like a sex object, Adrian, and he expected his evening meal cooked for him, and he cut his toe-nails in the living room, and besides I'm very fond of your father". She didn't mention me.

Wednesday December 16th

I am in an experimental Nativity play* at school. It is called *Manger* to Star*. I am playing Joseph. Pandora is playing Mary. Jesus is played by the smallest first-year. He is called Peter Brown. He is on drugs to make him taller.

to intercept *G.* abfangen **soggy** unpleasantly wet **to focus** ['fəʊkəs] **on** to concentrate on **Nativity** [nə'tɪvətɪ] **play** a play about the birth of Jesus Christ with young children as actors **manger** ['meɪndʒə] crib (*G.* Krippe)

Thursday December 17th

Another letter from the BBC!

Dear Adrian Mole,

Thank you for submitting your latest poem. I understood it perfectly well once it had been typed. However, Adrian, understanding is not all. Our Poetry Department is inundated* with Autumnal poems. The smell of bonfires and the crackling of leaves pervade* the very corridors. Good try, but try again, eh?

Yours with Best Wishes,

John Tydeman

"Try again"! He is almost giving me a commission*. I have written back to him:

Dear Mr Tydeman,

How much will I get if you broadcast one of my poems on the radio? When do you want me to send it? What do you want it to be about? Can I read it out myself? Will you pay my train fare in advance*? What time will it go out on the airways? I have to be in bed by ten.

Yours faithfully,

A. Mole

P.S. I hope you have a dead good Christmas.

Friday December 18th

MOON'S LAST QUARTER

Today's rehearsal* of *Manger to Star* was a fiasco. Peter Brown has grown too big for the crib, so Mr Animba, the Woodwork teacher, has got to make another one.

Mr Scruton sat at the back of the gym and watched rehearsals. He had a face like the north face of the Eiger* by the time we'd got to the bit where the three wise men were reviled* as capitalist pigs.

He took Miss Elf into the showers and had a "Quiet Word". We all heard every word he shouted. He said he wanted to see a traditional Nativity play, with a Tiny* Tears doll* playing Jesus and three wise men dressed in dressing gowns and tea towels. He threatened to cancel* the

to inundate ['ɪnʌndeɪt] *G.* überschwemmen **to pervade** *fml.* to spread through every part of **to give a commission** *fml.* to ask s.o. to do a special job **in advance** *G.* im Voraus **rehearsal** [rɪ'hɜːsl] *G.* Theaterprobe **Eiger** a mountain in central Switzerland **to revile** *fml.* to insult, to curse **tiny** very small **doll** *G.* Puppe **to cancel** *here: G.* absetzen

play if Mary, alias Pandora, continued to go into simulated labour* in the manger. This is typical of Scruton, he is nothing but a small-minded, provincial, sexually-inhibited* fascist pig. How he rose to become a headmaster I do not know. He has been wearing the same hairy green suit for three years. How can we change it all now? The play is being performed on Tuesday afternoon.

My mother has had a Cristmas card from creep Lucas! Inside he had written, "Paulie, Have you got the dry-cleaning ticket for my best white suit? Sketchley's are being very difficult". My mother was very upset. My father rang Sheffield and ordered Lucas to cease* communications, or risk getting a bit of Sheffield steel in between his porky* shoulder blades*. My father looked dead good on the telephone. He had a cigarette stuck between his lips. My mother was leaning on the corner of the fridge. She had a cigarette in her hand. They looked a bit like the Humphrey Bogart* and Lauren Bacall* postcard on my wall. I wish I was a *real* gangster's son, at least you would see a bit of life.

Saturday December 19th

I've got no money for Christmas presents. But I have made my Christmas list in case I find ten pounds in the street.

Pandora—Big bottle of Chanel Nr. 5 (£ 1.50)
Mother—Egg-timer (75 p)
Father—Bookmark (38 p)
Grandma—Packet of J cloths* (43 p)
Dog—Dog chocolates (45 p)
Bert—20 Woodbines (95 p)
Auntie Susan—Tin of Nivea (60 p)
Sabre—Box of Bob Martins*, small (39 p)
Nigel—Family box of Maltesers* (34 p)
Miss Elf—Oven-glove (home-made)

labour *here: G.* Geburtswehen **inhibited** [ɪnˈhɪbɪtɪd] *G.* gehemmt **to cease** [siːs] to stop **porky** *inf.* fat **shoulder blade** *G.* Schulterblatt **Humphrey Bogart** (1899–1957)/**Lauren Bacall** (born 1924) famous American film stars, played in a lot of gangster films **J cloth** (trademark) a cloth for cleaning plates, cups, etc **Bob Martin** (trademark) dog food **Malteser** (trademark) round chocolates

Sunday December 20th

FOURTH IN ADVENT

Pandora and I had a private Mary and Joseph rehearsal in my bedroom. We improvised a great scene where Mary gets back from the Family Planning Clinic and tells Joseph she's pregnant*. I played Joseph like Marlon Brando* in *A Streetcar Named Desire**. Pandora played Mary a bit like Blanche Dubois*; it was dead good until my father complained about the shouting. The dog was supposed to be the lowly* cattle, but it wouldn't keep still long enough to make a tableau*.

After tea my mother casually mentioned that she was going to wear her fox-fur coat to the school concert tomorrow. Shock! Horror! I immediately went round to Pandora's house to get the mangy* coat, only to find that Pandora's mother has borrowed it to go to the Marriage Guidance* Christmas dinner and dance! Pandora said that she hadn't realized that the coat was only on loan*; she thought it was a lover's gift*! How can a 14 3/4-year-old schoolboy afford to give a fox-fur coat as a gift? Who does Pandora think I am, a millionaire like Freddie Laker*?

Pandora's mother won't be back until the early hours so I will have to go round before school and sneak the coat into its plastic cover. It's going to be difficult, but then nothing in my life is simple or straightforward any more. I feel like a character in a Russian novel half the time.

Monday December 21st

Woke up with a panic attack to see that it was eight-fifty by my bedside digital! My black walls looked unusually light and sparkly*; one glance outside confirmed* my suspicions that indeed the snow lay outside like a white carpet.

I stumbled* through the snow to Pandora's house in my father's fishing boots but found that the house was devoid of* humans. I looked through the letterbox and saw my mother's fur coat being mauled about* by Pandora's ginger cat. I shouted swear-words at it but the lousy stink-

pregnant *G.* schwanger **A Streetcar Named Desire** a play by Tennessee Williams (1947), made into a film with **Marlon Brando** as Stanley Kowalski, a brutish man, who quarrels endlessly with his wife's lonely and sensitive sister, **Blanche Dubois** **lowly** simple, inferior **tableau** ['tæbləʊ] a scene where nobody moves on stage **mangy** *G.* schäbig **Marriage Guidance** *G.* Eheberatungsstelle **to be on loan** to be borrowed **gift** present **Freddie Laker** director of a popular and cheap airline service from 1982 to 1983 **sparkly** *inf.* brilliant **to confirm** *G.* bestätigen **to stumble** *G.* stolpern **devoid of** without **to maul about** *here:* to play roughly with, to drag about

ing cat just looked sarcastic and carried on dragging the coat around the hall. I had no choice but to shoulder-charge* the laundry-room door and rush into the hall and rescue my mother's coat. I left quickly (as quickly as anyone can wearing thigh-length* fishing boots, four sizes too big). I put the fur coat on to keep me warm on my hazardous* journey home. I nearly lost my bearings* at the corner of Ploughman's Avenue and Shepherd's Crook Drive, but I fought my way through the blizzard* until I saw the familiar sight of the prefabricated* garages on the corner of our cul-de-sac.

I fell into our kitchen in a state of hypothermia and severe exhaustion*; my mother was smoking a cigarette and making mince pies*. She screamed, "What the bloody hell are you doing wearing my fox-fur coat?" She was not kind or concerned or anything that mothers are supposed to be. She fussed about*, wiping snow off the coat and drying the fur with a hair dryer. She didn't even offer to make me a hot drink or anything. She said, "It's been on the radio that the school is closed because of the snow, so you can make yourself useful and check the camp beds for rust. The Sugdens are staying over Christmas." The Sugdens! My mother's relations from Norfolk*! Yuk*, Yuk. They are all inbred* and can't speak properly!

Phoned Pandora to explain about the fox-fur and the damage, etc., but she had gone skiing on the slope* behind the Co-op bakery. Pandora's father asked me to get off the line, he had to make an urgent phone call to the police station. He said he had just come home and discovered a break-in! He said the place was a shambles* (the cat must have done it, I was very careful), but fortunately the only thing that was missing was an old fox-fur coat that Pandora had lined the cat's basket with.

Sorry Pandora, but this is the final straw that broke the donkey's back*! You can find yourself another Joseph, I refuse to share the stage with a girl who puts her cat's comfort before her boyfriend's dilemma.

to shoulder-charge to push hard with your schoulder **thigh-length** *G.* bis zu den Oberschenkeln reichend **hazardous** ['hæzədəs] dangerous **to lose one's bearings** to lose one's way **blizzard** a very bad snow storm **prefabricated** [ˌpriːˈfæbrɪkeɪtɪd] *G.* vorgefertigt **exhaustion** [ɪgˈzɔːstʃən] extreme tiredness **mince pie** *G.* mit Dörrobst und Sirup gefülltes süßes Gebäck **to fuss about** to behave in a nervous way **Norfolk** [ˈnɔːfək] a county on the East coast of England **yuk** *sl.* (showing that one does not like s.th.) **inbred** having ancestors (*G.* Vorfahren) who were all relatives of each other **slope** *G.* Abhang **to be a shambles** to be a total mess **the final straw that breaks the camel's neck** *fig. G.* der Tropfen, der das Fass zum Überlaufen bringt **donkey** *G.* Esel

Tuesday December 22nd

School was closed this morning because the teachers couldn't manage to get in on time because of the snow. That will teach them to live in old mill houses and windmills out in the country! Miss Elf lives with a West Indian in a terraced house* in the town, so she bravely turned out to prepare for the school concert in the afternoon. I decided to forgive Pandora for the fox-fur in the cat's basket incident after she had pointed out that the cat was an expectant* mother.

The school concert was not a success. The bell ringing from class One-G went on too long, my father said "The Bells! The Bells!", and my mother laughed too loudly and made Mr. Scruton look at her.

The school orchestra was a disaster! My mother said, "When are they going to stop tuning-up* and start playing?" I told her that they had just played a Mozart horn concerto. That made my mother and father and Pandora's mother and father start laughing in a very unmannerly fashion. When ten-stone* Alice Bernard from Three-C came on stage in a tutu* and did the dying swan I thought my mother would explode. Alice Bernard's mother led the applause, but not many people followed.

The Dumbo* class got up and sang a few boring old carols*. Barry Kent sang all the vulgar versions (I know because I was watching his lips) then they sat down cross-legged, and brainbox Henderson from Five-K played a trumpet, Jew's harp*, piano and guitar. The smarmy git looked dead superior* when he was bowing during his applause. Then it was the interval and time for me to change into my white-T-shirt-and-Wranglers Joseph costume. The tension* backstage* was electric. I stood in the wings (a theatrical term—it means the side of the stage) and watched the audience filing* back into their places. Then the music from *Close Encounters** boomed out over the stereo speakers, and the curtains opened on an abstract manger and I just had time to whisper to Pandora "Break a leg, darling", before Miss Elf pushed us out into the lights. My performance was brilliant! I really got under the skin of Joseph but Pandora was less good, she forgot to look tenderly* at Jesus/Peter Brown.

terraced ['terəst] **house** *G.* Reihenhaus **expectant** *here:* future **to tune-up** to adjust music instruments **stone** *here:* 6.35 kilograms **tutu** ['tu:tu:] a costume worn by female ballet dancers **dumbo** *inf.* stupid **carol** a traditional Christmas song **Jew's harp** *G.* Maultrommel **superior** [su:'pɪərɪə] *here:* arrogant **tension** *G.* Spannung **backstage** the area behind the stage **to file** to walk one behind the other **Close Encounters (of the Third Kind)** a 1977 science fiction film by Stephen Spielberg **tender** loving, caring

The three punks/wise men made too much noise with their chains* and spoiled* my speech* about the Middle East situation, and the angels representing* Mrs Thatcher got hissed* by the audience so loudly that their spoken chorus about unemployment was wasted.

Still, all in all, it was well received by the audience. Mr Scruton got up and made a hypocritical* speech about "a brave experiment" and "Miss Elf's tireless work behind the scenes", and then we all sang "We wish you a Merry Christmas"!

Driving home in the car my father said, "That was the funniest Nativity play I have ever seen. Whose idea was it to turn it into a comedy?" I didn't reply. It wasn't a comedy.

Wednesday December 23rd

9 a.m. Only two shopping days left for Christmas and I am still penniless. I have made a *Blue Peter* oven-glove for Miss Elf, but in order to give it to her in time for Christmas I will have to go into the ghetto* and risk getting mugged*.

I will have to go out carol singing, there is nothing else I can do to raise finance*.

10 p.m. Just got back from carol singing. The suburban houses were a dead loss. People shouted, "Come back at Christmas", without even opening the door. My most appreciative* audience were the drunks staggering in and out of the Black Bull. Some of them wept openly at the beauty of my solo rendition* of "Silent Night". I must say that I presented a touching* picture as I stood in the snow with my young face lifted to the heavens ignoring the scenes of drunken revelry* around me.

I made £ 3.13 ½ plus an Irish tenpence and Guinness bottletop. I'm going out again tomorrow. I will wear my school uniform, it should be worth a few extra quid*.

chain *G.* Kette **to spoil** to ruin **speech** *G.* Ansprache, Rede **to represent** to be a sign for s.th. **to hiss** to make a sound like a sharp "s" to show that one does not like s.th. **hypocritical** [ˌhɪpəʊ'krɪtɪkl] *contempt.* not showing what one really feels **ghetto** ['getəʊ] *here contempt.* the part of a town where many poor people live in isolation from other people **to mug** *inf.* to attack, to rob **to raise finance** to get/collect money **appreciative** [ə'priːʃjətɪv] pleased, thankful **rendition** [ren'dɪʃn] performance, *here:* singing **touching** *G.* rührend **revelry** ['revlrɪ] noisy and drunken party **quid** *inf.* [kwɪd] a British pound sterling

Thursday December 24th

Took Bert's Woodbines round to the home. Bert is hurt because I haven't been to see him. He said he didn't want to spend Christmas with a lot of malicious* old women. Him and Queenie are causing a scandal. They are unofficially engaged*. They have got their names on the same ashtray. I have invited Bert and Queenie for Christmas Day. My mother doesn't know yet but I'm sure she won't mind, we have got a big turkey. I sang a few carols for the old ladies. I made two pounds eleven pence out of them so I went to Woolworth's to buy Pandora's Chanel No. 5. They hadn't got any so I bought her an underarm deodorant instead.

The house looks dead clean and sparkling, there is a magic smell of cooking and satsumas* in the air. I have searched around for my presents but they are not in the usual place. I want a racing bike, nothing else will please me. It's time I was independently* mobile.

11 p.m. Just got back from the Black Bull. Pandora came with me, we wore our school uniforms and reminded all the drunk of their own children. They coughed up* conscience money to the tune of* twelve pounds fifty-seven! So we are going to see a pantomime on Boxing Day* and we will have a family bar of Cadbury's Dairy Milk each!

Friday December 25th
CHRISTMAS DAY

Got up at 5 a.m. to have a ride on my racing bike. My father paid for it with American Express. I couldn't ride it far because of the snow, but it didn't matter. I just like looking at it. My father had written on the gift tag attached* to the handlebars, "Don't leave it out in the rain this time"— as if I would!

My parents had severe hangovers, so I took them breakfast in bed and gave them my presents at the same time. My mother was overjoyed with her egg-timer and my father was equally delighted with his bookmark, in fact everything was going OK until I casually* mentioned that Bert and Queenie were my guests for the day, and would my father mind getting out of bed and picking them up in his car.

malicious [mə'lɪʃəs] wanting to do harm **to be engaged** *here:* having promised to marry **satsuma** ['sætsʊmə] a small citrus fruit that looks like an orange **independent** *here:* free **to cough up** *inf.* to give **to the tune of** *here: G.* in Höhe von **Boxing Day** the 26th of December **to attach** [ə'tætʃ] to fasten **casually** ['kæʒjʊəlɪ] *G.* beiläufig

The row went on until the lousy Sugdens arrived. My grandma and grandad Sugden and Uncle Dennis and his wife Marcia and their son Maurice all look the same, as if they went to funerals* every day of their lives. I can hardly believe that my mother is related to them. The Sugdens refused a drink and had a cup of tea whilst my mother defrosted* the turkey in the bath. I helped my father carry Queenie (fifteen stone) and Bert (fourteen stone) out of our car. Queenie is one of those loud types of old ladies who dye* their hair and try to look young. Bert is in love with her. He told me when I was helping him into the toilet.

Grandma Mole and Auntie Susan came at twelve-thirty and pretended to like the Sugdens. Auntie Susan told some amusing stories about life in prison but nobody but me and my father and Bert and Queenie laughed.

I went up to the bathroom and found my mother crying and running the turkey under the hot tap. She said, "The bloody thing won't thaw out, Adrian. What am I going to do?" I said, "Just bung* it in the oven". So she did.

We sat down to eat Christmas dinner four hours late. By then my father was too drunk to eat anything. The Sugdens enjoyed the Queen's Speech* but nothing else seemed to please them. Grandma Sugden gave me a book called *Bible Stories for Boys*. I could hardly tell her that I had lost my faith*, so I said thank-you and wore a false smile for so long that it hurt.

The Sugdens went to their camp beds at ten o'clock. Bert, Queenie and my mother and father played cards while I polished* my bike. We all had a good time making jokes about the Sugdens. Then my father drove Bert and Queenie back to the home and I phoned Pandora up and told her that I loved her more than life itself.

I am going round to her house tomorrow to give her the deodorant and escort* her to the pantomime*.

funeral ['fjuːnərəl] *G.* Begräbnis **to defrost** *G.* auf-, abtauen **to dye** to change the colour of s.th. **to bung** *inf.* to put s.th. quickly somewhere **speech** *here: G.* Weihnachtsansprache (on TV) **faith** belief **to polish** *here:* to make s.th. shine, to clean **to escort** [–'–] to go with **pantomime** *BE* a funny musical play (traditionally a fairy tale story) shown at Christmas

Saturday December 26th

BANK HOLIDAY IN UK AND REP. OF IRELAND (a day may be given in lieu*). NEW MOON

The Sugdens got up at 7 a.m. and sat around in their best clothes looking respectable. I went out on my bike. When I got back my mother was still in bed, and my father was arguing with Grandad Sugden about our dog's behaviour, so I went for another ride.

I called in on Grandma Mole, ate four mince pies, then rode back home. I got up to 30 mph on the dual carriageway*, it was dead good. I put my new suede jacket and corduroy trousers on (courtesy of* my father's Barclaycard) and called for Pandora; she gave me a bottle of aftershave for my Christmas present. It was a proud moment, it signified* the *End of Childhood.*

We quite enjoyed the pantomime but it was rather childish for our taste. Bill Ash and Carole Hayman were good as Aladdin and the Princess, but the robbers played by Jeff Teare and Ian Giles were best. Sue Pomeroy gave a hilarious* performance as Widow* Twankey*. In this she was greatly helped by her cow, played by Chris Martin and Lou Wakefield.

Sunday December 27th

1ST AFTER CHRISTMAS

The Sugdens have gone back to Norfolk, thank God!

The house is back to its usual mess. My parents took a bottle of vodka and two glasses to bed with them last night. I haven't seen them since.

Went to Melton Mowbray on my bike, did it in five hours.

Monday December 28th

I am in trouble for leaving my bike outside last night. My parents are not speaking to me. I don't care, I have just had a shave and I feel magic.

in lieu [ljuː] *fml.* in place of, instead of **dual carriageway** *BE G.* (vierspurige) Schnellstraße **courtesy** [ˈkɜːtɪsɪ] **of** *fml.* thanks to **to signify** *here:* to show, to mean **hilarious** [hɪˈleərɪəs] extremely funny **widow** a woman whose husband has died **Widow Twankey** (in British pantomimes:) Aladdin's wild mother

Tuesday December 29th

My father is in a bad mood because there is only a bottle of V.P. sherry left to drink. He has gone round to Pandora's house to borrow a bottle of spirits.

The dog has pulled the Christmas tree down and made all the pine* needles stick in the shag-pile*.

I have finished all my Christmas books and the library is still shut. I am reduced to* reading my father's *Reader's Digests* and testing my word power.

Wednesday December 30th

All the balloons have shrivelled* up. They look like old women's breasts shown on television documentaries about the Third World.

Thursday December 31st

The last day of the year! A lot has happened. I have fallen in love. Been a one-parent child. Gone Intellectual. And had two letters from the BBC. Not bad going for a 14 3/4-year-old!

My mother and father have been to a New Year's Eve dance at the Grand Hotel. My mother actually wore a dress! It is over a year since she showed her legs in public.

Pandora and I saw the New Year in together, we had a dead passionate session* accompanied by Andy Stewart and a bag-piper*.

My father came crashing through the front door at 1 a.m. carrying a lump of coal* in his hand. Drunk as usual.

My mother started going on about what a wonderful son I was and how much she loved me. It's a pity she never says anthing like that when she is sober*.

pine *G.* Kiefer **shag** carpet **pile** *here: G.* Flor **to be reduced to** *here:* to be forced to **to shrivel up** to become smaller by drying out **session** *here:* period of time, meeting **bag-piper** *G.* Dudelsackspieler **lump of coal** *here:* a piece of coal (carried into the house as a symbol of a happy new year) **sober** ['səʊbə] not drunk

Friday January 1st
BANK HOLIDAY IN UK, REP. OF IRELAND, USA AND CANADA

These are my New Year's resolutions:

1. I will be true to Pandora.
2. I will bring my bike in at night.
3. I will not read unworthy* books.
4. I will study hard for my O levels, and get Grade* "A"s.
5. I will try to be more kind to the dog.
6. I will try to find it in my heart to forgive Barry Kent his multiple* sins.
7. I will clean the bath after use.
8. I will stop worrying about the size of my thing.
9. I will do my back-stretching exercises every night without fail.
10. I will learn a new word and use it every day.

Saturday January 2nd
BANK HOLIDAY IN SCOTLAND (a day may be given in lieu)

How interesting it is that Aabec should be an Australian bark* used for making sweat.

Sunday January 3rd
SECOND AFTER CHRISTMAS. MOON'S FIRST QUARTER

I wouldn't mind going to Africa and hunting an Aardvark*.

Monday January 4th

Whilst in Africa I would go South and look out for an Aardwolf*.

Tuesday January 5th

And I would avoid tangling* with an Aasvogel*.

unworthy *G.* unwürdig **grade** *here:* mark **multiple** *here:* many **bark** *G.* Rinde **Aardvark** ['ɑːdvɑːk] *Afrikaans* antbear *G.* Erdferkel (lives on insects) **Aardwolf** ['ɑːdwʊlf] *Afrikaans* an African animal that looks like a small striped hyena **to tangle** *here:* to fight **Aasvogel** *arch. Afrikaans* vulture *G.* Aasgeier

Wednesday January 6th
EPIPHANY

I keep having nightmares about the bomb. I hope it isn't dropped before I get my GCE results in August 1983. I wouldn't like to die an unqualified virgin*.

Thursday January 7th

Nigel came round to look at my racing bike. He said that it was mass produced, unlike his bike that was "made by a craftsman* in Nottingham". I have gone off* Nigel, and I have also gone off my bike a bit.

Friday January 8th

Got a wedding invitation from Bert and Queenie, they are getting married on January 16th at Pocklington Street Register Office*.

In my opinion it is a waste of time. Bert is nearly ninety and Queenie is nearly eighty. I will leave it until the last minute before I buy a wedding present.

It has started snowing again. I asked my mother to buy me some green wellingtons like the Queen's but she came back with dead common black ones. I only need them to walk Pandora to our gate. I am staying in until the snow melts. Unlike most youths of my age, I dislike frolicking* in the snow.

Saturday January 9th
FULL MOON

Nigel said the end of the world is coming tonight. He said the moon is having a total collapse*. (Nigel should read *Reader's Digest* and increase* his word power.) True enough it did go dark, I held my breath and feared the worst but then the moon recovered and life went on as usual, except in York* where fate* has flooded the town centre.

virgin s.o. without sexual experience **craftsman** ['krɑːftsmən] s.o. who is trained in a job where people have to work with their hands **to go off** *inf.* to stop liking **register office** (registry) *here: G.* Standesamt **to frolic** to play and jump about happily **collapse** Nigel is confusing the words "eclipse" (*G.* Mondfinsternis) and "collapse" (*G.* Zusammenbruch) **to increase** to make larger **York** a city in North East England **fate** *G.* Schicksal

Sunday January 10th
FIRST AFTER EPIPHANY

I can't understand why my father looks so old at forty-one compared to President Reagan at seventy. My father has got no work or worries yet he looks dead haggard*. Poor President Reagan has to carry the world's safety on his shoulders yet he is always smiling and looking cheerful. It doesn't make sense.

Monday January 11th

I've been looking through last year's diary and have been reminded that Malcolm Muggeridge never did reply to my letter about what to do if you are an intellectual. That is a first-class* stamp wasted! I should have written to the British Museum, that's where all the intellectuals hang out*.

Tuesday January 12th

Pandora and I went to the youth club tonight. It was quite good. Rick Lemon led a discussion on sex. Nobody said anything, but he showed some interesting slides* of wombs* cut in half.

Wednesday January 13th

Pandora's parents have had a massive row. They are sleeping in separate bedrooms. Pandora's mother has joined the SDP* and Pandora's father is staying loyal to the Labour Party.

Pandora is a Liberal*, so she gets on all right with them both.

Thursday January 14th

Pandora's father has come out of the closet* and admitted that he is a Bennite*. Pandora is staying loyal to him, but if the Co-op Dairy find out he will be finished.

haggard looking tired and old in one's face **first-class** a quicker and more expensive way of sending letters and postcards by post **to hang out** *inf.* to spend a lot of time somewhere **slide** *G.* Dia **womb** [wu:m] the part inside a woman's body where the baby grows before it is born **SDP** (Social Democratic Party) formed in 1981 by some former Labour Party politicians **liberal** moderate, tolerant **Liberal Party** a moderate British party, has by now gone together with the SDP **to come out of the closet** to show that you have a particular belief which you kept secret before **Bennite** a follower of Tony Benn, a left-wing and critical member of the Labour Party

Friday January 15th

Thank God the snow is melting! At last I can walk the streets in safety, secure in the knowledge that no one is going to ram* a snowball down the back of my anorak.

Saturday January 16th
MOON'S LAST QUARTER

Bert got married today.

The Alderman Cooper Sunshine Home hired a coach and took the old ladies to form a guard of honour with their walking-frames*.

Bert looked dead good. He cashed his life insurance* in and spent the money on a new suit. Queenie was wearing a hat made of flowers and fruit. She had a lot of orange make-up on her face to try and cover the wrinkles*. Even Sabre had a red bow round his neck. I think it was kind of the RSPCA to let Sabre out for his master's wedding. My father and Pandora's father carried Bert's wheelchair up the steps with Bert a single man and then down again with Bert a married man. The old ladies threw rice and confetti and my mother and Pandora's mother gave Queenie a kiss and a lucky horseshoe.

A newspaper reporter and photographer made everyone pose for photographs. I was asked my name, but I said I didn't want publicity for my acts of charity* to Bert.

The reception took place back at the home. Matron made a cake with "B" and "Q" written in Jellytots*.

Bert and Queenie are moving into a bungalow on Monday, after they have had their honeymoon in the home.

Honeymoon! Ha! Ha! Ha!

Sunday January 17th
SECOND AFTER EPIPHANY

Last night I dreamed about a boy like me collecting pebbles in the rain. It was a dead strange dream.

I am reading *The Black Prince**, by Iris Murdoch*. I can only under-

to ram to push with great force **frame** *G.* 1. Rahmen 2. Gestell **life insurance** *G.* Lebensversicherung **wrinkle** a line in one's skin, especially on one's face **act of charity** ['tʃærɪtɪ] *G.* Akt der Nächstenliebe **Jellytots** (trademark) small sweets **The Black Prince** (1973) a novel by **Iris Murdoch**, a demanding novelist and philosopher

stand one word in ten. It is now my ambition* to actually enjoy one of her books. Then I will know I am above the common herd.

Monday January 18th

School. First day of term. Loads of GCE homework. I will never cope*. I am an intellectual but at the same time I am not very clever.

Tuesday January 19th

Brought four hundred and eighty-three copies of *The Voice of Youth* home in my satchel and Adidas bag. Mr Jones needs the games cupboard.

Wednesday January 20th

Two-and-a-half hours of homework! I will crack under the strain.

Thursday January 21st

My brain is hurting. I have just had two pages of *Macbeth** to translate* into English.

Friday January 22nd

I am destined* to become a manual* worker. I can't keep working under this pressure. Miss Elf said my work is perfectly satisfactory, but that isn't good enough when Pandora keeps getting "Excellent" in red pen on everything she does.

Saturday January 23rd

Stayed in bed until five-thirty to make sure I missed Sainsbury's. Listened to Radio Four play about domestic* unhappiness. Phoned Pandora. Did Geography homework. Teased* dog. Went to sleep. Woke up. Worried for ten minutes. Got up. Made cocoa.

I am a nervous wreck.

ambition desire to be successful, dream **to cope** to manage, to deal with successfully **Macbeth** (1606) a tragedy by William Shakespeare (1564–1616), written in an older form of today's English **to translate** *G.* übersetzen **to destine** ['destɪn] *G.* (vorher)bestimmen **manual** ['mænjʊəl] *here:* using the hands **domestic** at home **to tease** *G.* ärgern, necken

Sunday January 24th
THIRD AFTER EPIPHANY

My mother blames my bad nerves on Iris Murdoch. She says painful adolescence shouldn't be read about when one is studying for O levels.

Monday January 25th
NEW MOON

Couldn't do my Maths homework. Phoned the Samaritans. The nice man on the end of the phone told me the answer was nine-eighths. He was dead kind to someone in despair.

Tuesday January 26th

The stupid Samaritan got the answer wrong! It's only seven-fifths. I only got six out of twenty. Pandora got them all right. In fact she got a hundred per cent.

Wednesday January 27th

My mother is holding her woman's rights meetings in our lounge. I can't concentrate on my homework properly with women laughing and shouting and stamping up the stairs. They are not a bit ladylike.

Thursday January 28th

Got fifteen out of twenty for History. Pandora got twenty-one out of twenty. She got an extra mark for knowing Hitler's father's name.

Friday January 29th

Came home from school early with a severe migraine (missed the Comparative Religion test). Found my father watching *Play School* and pretending to be an acorn* growing into an oak*.

Went to bed too shocked to speak.

Saturday January 30th

Migraine. Too ill to write.

acorn ['eɪkɔːn] *G.* Eichel **oak** *G.* Eiche

Sunday January 31st
FOURTH AFTER EPIPHANY

Pandora came round. I copied her homework. Feel better.

Monday February 1st
MOON'S FIRST QUARTER

My mother has given my father an ultimatum: either he finds a job, or starts doing housework, or leaves.

He is looking for a job.

Tuesday February 2nd
CANDLEMAS (SCOTTISH QUARTER-DAY)

Grandma Mole came to tell me that the end of the world was announced at her Spiritualist church last week. She said it should have all ended yesterday.

She would have come round sooner only she was washing her curtains.

Wednesday February 3rd

My father has had his credit cards taken off him! Barclays, Nat West and American Express have got fed up with his reckless* spending. Time is running out for us. He has only got a few quid's redundancy money left in his sock drawer.

My mother is looking for a job.

I have got a sense of *déjà vu**.

Thursday February 4th

Went round to see Bert and Queenie. Their bungalow is so full of knick-knacks* that there is hardly room for a person to move. Sabre knocks at least ten things over every time he wags* his tail*. They both seem happy enough, though their sex life can't be up to much.

Friday February 5th

I've got to write an essay on the causes of the Second World War. What a waste of time! Everyone knows the causes. You can't go anywhere without seeing Hitler's photo.

reckless *here:* foolish, careless **déjà vu** ['deɪʒæ 'vu:] *French* the feeling that one has already seen s.th. that is now happening all over again **knick-knacks** small objects to look at or play with **to wag** to move from side to side **tail** *G.* Schwanz

Saturday February 6th

Finished essay; copied it out of *Pear's Encyclopedia.*

My mother has gone to a woman's workshop on self-defence. So if my father moans at her for burning the toast she will be able to karate-chop* him in the windpipe*.

Sunday February 7th

SEPTUAGESIMA

Bored stiff* all day. My parents never do anything on Sundays but read the Sunday papers. Other families go out to safari parks, etc. But we never do.

When I am a parent I will fill my children with stimulation at weekends.

Monday February 8th

FULL MOON

My mother has found a job. She collects money from Space Invader machines. She started today in response* to an urgent phone call from the job agency* that she is registered with*.

She said that the fullest machines are those in unrespectable cafés and university common rooms*.

I think my mother is betraying* her principles. She is pandering* to an obsession* of weak minds.

Tuesday February 9th

My mother has given up her job. She said she is sexually harassed* during her work and she is also allergic to ten-pence pieces.

to karate-chop to cut with a karate movement of one's hands **windpipe** *G.* Luftröhre **to be bored stiff** *inf.* to be extremely bored **response** answer **job agency** *G.* (private) Arbeitsvermittlung **to be registered with** *G.* eingetragen sein bei **university common rooms** rooms where students spend their spare time, drinking coffee, etc. **to betray** to be disloyal to **to pander to** *contempt.* to fulfill people's wishes even if it is not good for them **obsession** *G.* Besessenheit; Zwangsvorstellung **to harass** ['hærəs] to trouble, to annoy

Wednesday February 10th

My father is going to start his own business making spice-racks*. He has spent the last of his redundancy money on buying pine and glue*. Our spare bedroom has been turned into a workshop. Sawdust* is all over the house.

I am very proud of my father. He is now a company director, and I am a company director's son!

Thursday February 11th

Delivered* Mrs Singh's massive spice-rack after school. It took two of us to carry it round and install it* on her kitchen wall. We had a cup of sickly Indian tea and Mrs Singh paid my father and then started to fill up her shelves with exotic Indian spices. They looked a lot more interesting than my mother's boring parsley* and thyme*.

My father bought a bottle of champagne to celebrate his first sale! He has got no respect for capital investment.

Friday February 12th

Pandora has gone to London with her father to hear Tony Benn speak. Pandora's mother has gone to a SDP rally* in Loughborough. It is a sad day when families are split by politics.

I'm not sure how I will vote. Sometimes I think Mrs Thatcher is a nice kind sort of woman. Then the next day I see her on television and she frightens me rigid*. She has got eyes like a psychotic* killer, but a voice like a gentle person. It is a bit confusing.

Saturday February 13th

Pandora has got a crush on* Tony Benn*, just like the one she had on Adam Ant. She says that older men are exciting.

I am trying to grow my moustache. Valentine's Day tomorrow. A big card came today, it had a Sheffield postmark.

spicerack *G.* Gewürzregal **glue** *G.* Klebstoff **sawdust** *G.* Sägemehl **to deliver** to take s. th. (e. g. a letter) to another person or place **to install** to put in a place **parsley** *G.* Petersilie **thyme** [taɪm] *G.* Thymian **rally** a large public meeting **to frighten s. o. rigid** ['rɪdʒɪd] *inf.* to give s. o. a serious shock **psychotic** [saɪ'kɒtɪk] *medical expression* mad, insane **to have a crush on** to feel a strong love for **Tony Benn** (born 1925) an important left-wing member of the Labour Party; himself the son of a viscount, he refused to accept his father's title

Sunday February 14th
SEXAGESIMA. ST VALENTINE'S DAY

At last I have had a valentine from somebody who is not a blood relation! Pandora's card was charming, she had written a simple message of love:

Adrian, it is you alone.

I gave Pandora a false Victorian* card, inside I wrote:

My young love,
Treacle hair and knee-socks
Give my system deep shocks.
You've got a magic figure:
I'm Roy Rogers*, you are Trigger*.

It doesn't scan* very well, but I was in a hurry. Pandora didn't get the literary reference* to Roy Rogers, so I have lent her my father's old Roy Rogers annuals*.

My father threw the Sheffield card in the waste-bin. My mother took it out when my father had gone to the pub. Inside it said:

Pauline, I am in anguish*.

My mother smiled and ripped* it up.

Monday February 15th
WASHINGTON'S BIRTHDAY, USA. MOON'S LAST QUARTER

Came home from school to hear my mother talking to creep Lucas on the phone. She was using a yukky voice and saying things like: "Don't ask me to do it, Bimbo", and "It's all over between us now, darling. We must try to forget".

I can't stand much more emotional* stress. I am up to my ears in it already what with studying hard and vying* with Tony Benn for Pandora's attention.

Tuesday February 16th

Pandora's mother came round last night to complain about her spice-rack. It fell off the wall and spilt rosemary and tumeric* all over her cork

Victorian belonging to the 19th century, esp. when Queen Victoria was Queen of England (1837–1901!) **to scan** *G.* sich reimen **Roy Rogers** a TV cowboy hero of the 1940's and 1950's whose horse was called **Trigger**. **reference** *here:* hint **annual** *G.* Jahrbuch **anguish** very great pain **to rip up** to tear into pieces **emotional** *here: G.* gefühlsmäßig **to vie** [vaɪ] **with** to compete with **tumeric** (correctly: turmeric) ['tɜːmərɪk] *G.* Kurkuma, Gelbwurzel

tiles*. My mother apologized* on behalf of* my father who was hiding in the coal shed.

I am seriously thinking of giving everything up and running away to be a tramp. I would quite enjoy the life, providing I could have a daily bath.

Wednesday February 17th

Miss Elf told us about her boyfriend today. He is called Winston Johnson. He is a Master of Arts* and can't get a job! So what chance do I stand?

Miss Elf said that school-leavers are despairing* all over the country. She said that Mr Scruton should be ashamed to have a portrait of Mrs Thatcher over his desk.

I think I am turning radical.

Thursday February 18th

This morning the whole school was ordered to go to the assembly hall. Mr Scruton got up on the stage and acted like the films of Hitler. He said in all his long years of teaching he had never come across an act of such serious vandalism. Everybody went dead quiet and wondered what had happened. Scruton said that somebody had entered his office and drawn a moustache on Margaret Thatcher and written "Three million unemployed" in her cleavage*.

He said that defiling* the greatest leader this country has ever known was a crime against humanity*. It was tantamount to* treason* and that when the culprit* was found they would be immediately expelled*. Scruton's eyes bulged out so far that a few of the first-years started to cry. Miss Elf led them outside to safety.

The whole school has got to have handwriting tests.

tile *G.* Fliese **to apologize** [ə'pɒlədʒaɪz] to say that one feels sorry **on behalf of** *here:* in the name of **Master of Arts** (M. A.) a university degree **to despair** to lose all hope **cleavage** ['kli:vɪdʒ] the space between a woman's breasts **to defile** *fml.* to make dirty **humanity** [hju:'mænətɪ] *here:* mankind, all people **tantamount** ['tæntəmaʊnt] **to** *fml.* having the same effect as **treason** an action against one's own country or government and in the interest of an enemy **culprit** s.o. who is guilty of a crime **to expel** to send away from, to dismiss

Friday February 19th

Miss Elf has resigned*. I will miss her, she was responsible* for my political development*. I am a committed* radical. I am against nearly everything.

Saturday February 20th

Pandora, Nigel, Claire Neilson and myself have formed a radical group. We are the "Pink Brigade". We discuss things like war (we are against it); peace (we are for it); and the ultimate* destruction* of capitalist society.

Claire Neilson's father is a capitalist; he owns a greengrocer's shop. Claire is trying to get her father to give cheap food to the unwaged* but he refuses. He waxes* fat on their starvation*!

Sunday February 21st
QUINQUAGESIMA

Had an argument with my father over the *Sunday Express*. He can't see that he is a willing tool of the reactionary* right. He refuses to change to the *Morning Star*. My mother reads anything; she is prostituting* her literacy*.

Monday February 22nd

Once again I am spotty. I am also extremely sexually frustrated. I'm sure a session of passionate lovemaking would improve my skin.

Pandora says she is not going to risk being a single parent just for the sake of* a few spots. So I will have to fall back on self-indulgence*.

to resign to give up (a job), to quit **responsible** *G.* verantwortlich **development** *G.* Entwicklung **committed** *here:* enthusiastic **ultimate** ['ʌltɪmət] final, last **destruction** breaking to pieces, being ruined **unwaged** (people) without a paid job **to wax** *fml.* to become **starvation** extreme hunger **reactionary** [rɪ'ækʃnərɪ] *contempt.* very conservative, trying to prevent all changes in society **to prostitute** ['prɒstɪtju:t] *fml. here:* to use s.th. badly to get money **literacy** ['lɪtərəsɪ] being able to read and write **for the sake of** because of **self–indulgence** *here:* giving oneself pleasure

Tuesday February 23rd
SHROVE TUESDAY. NEW MOON

Ate nine pancakes at home, three at Pandora's and four at Bert and Queenie's. Grandma was very hurt when I refused her kind offer to whip me a batter*, but I was full up.

It is disgusting when the Third World is living on a few grains* of rice.

I feel dead guilty.

Wednesday February 24th
ASH WEDNESDAY

Our school dinner-ladies have got the sack*! The dinners now come in hot boxes from a central kitchen. I would have staged* a protest but I have got a Geography test tomorrow.

Mrs Leech was presented with a microwave oven for her thirty years of toil* over the custard jug.

Thursday February 25th

Got fifteen out of twenty for Geography. I lost points for saying that the Falkland Islands* belonged to Argentina.

Friday February 26th

My thing is now thirteen centimetres long when it is extended*. When it is contracted* it is hardly worth measuring. My general physique* is improving. I think the back-stretching exercises are paying off. I used to be the sort of boy who had sand kicked in his face, now I'm the sort of boy who watches somebody else have it kicked in their face.

Saturday February 27th

My father hasn't made or sold a single spice-rack all week. We are now living on Social Security and dole money.

My mother has stopped smoking. The dog is down to half a tin of Chum a day.

to whip a batter to make a pancake quickly **grain** *G.* Korn **to get the sack** to become unemployed **to stage** *here:* to make **toil** *fml.* unpleasant and hard work **Falkland Islands** ['fɔːlklənd 'aɪləndz] a group of over 100 islands south of Argentina, with about 2,000 people, belonging to Britain though the Argentinians say that these islands should belong to their country **to extend** *here:* to become bigger (opposite: to **contract**) **physique** [fɪ'ziːk] *here:* the form of the male body

Sunday February 28th
QUADRAGESIMA (FIRST IN LENT)

Had egg and chips and peas for Sunday dinner! No pudding! Not even a proper serviette.

My mother says we are the *nouveaux** *poor.*

Monday March 1st
ST DAVID'S DAY (WALES)

My father has stopped smoking. He is going around with a white face finding fault* with everything I do.

My mother and him had their first row since she came back. The dog caused it by eating the Spam* for tea. It couldn't help it, the poor thing was half crazed* with hunger. It is back on a full tin of Chum a day.

Tuesday March 2nd
MOON'S FIRST QUARTER

My parents are suffering severe nicotine withdrawal* symptoms. It is quite amusing to a non-smoker like me.

Wednesday March 3rd

I had to lend my father enough money for a gallon of petrol, he had an interview for a job. My mother cut his hair and gave him a shave and told him what to say and how to behave. It is pathetic to see how unemployment has reduced my father to childish dependence* on others.

He is waiting to hear from Manpower Services.

He is still ill from not smoking. His temper* has reached new peaks* of explosion.

Thursday March 4th

No news yet about the job. I spend as much time as I can out of the house. My parents are unbearable*. I almost wish they would start smoking again.

nouveau ['nuːvəʊ] *French* (plural: noveaux) new **to find fault** to criticize **Spam** (trademark) pork meat in tins **to be half crazed** *inf.* to be almost mad **withdrawal** *here: G.* Entzug **dependence** *G.* Abhängigkeit **temper** *G.* Laune **peak** the highest point **unbearable** too unpleasant to accept or live with

Friday March 5th

He got it!!!

He starts on Monday as a Canal Bank Renovation Supervisor*. He is in charge of a gang of school-leavers. To celebrate he bought my mother sixty Benson and Hedges and himself sixty Players. I got a family pack of Mars bars.

Everybody is dead happy for once. Even the dog has cheered up a bit. Grandma is knitting my father a woolly hat for work.

Saturday March 6th

Pandora and I went to see the bit of canal bank that my father is now in charge of. If he worked for a thousand years he will never get it cleaned of all the old bikes and prams* and weeds* and Coca-Cola tins! I told my father that he was in a no-win situation, but he said, "On the contrary, in one year's time it will be a beauty spot". Yes! And I am Nancy Reagan*, Dad!

Sunday March 7th
SECOND IN LENT

My father went to see his canal bank this morning. He came home and shut himself in his bedroom. He is still there, I can hear my mother saying encouraging* words to him.

It is uncertain whether or not he will turn up for work tomorrow. On the whole I think not.

Monday March 8th

He went to work.

After school I walked home along the canal bank. I found him bossing* a gang of skinheads and punks about. They were looking surly* and uncooperative*. None of them wanted to get their clothes dirty. My father seemed to be the only one doing any work. He was covered in mud. I attempted* to exchange a few civilities* with the lads, but they

supervisor s.o. who is in charge of other people **pram** *G.* Kinderwagen **weed** an unwanted wild plant **Nancy Reagan** *cf. p. 96* **encouraging** giving hope **to boss** *inf.* to give orders to **surly** ['sɜːlɪ] being unfriendly and unwilling **uncooperative** [ˌʌnkəʊ'ɒpərətɪv] not willing to help **to attempt** to try **civilities** *here:* friendly and polite words

spurned my overtures*. I pointed out that the lads are alienated* by a cruel*, uncaring society, but my father said, "Bugger off* home, Adrian. You're talking a load of lefty* crap*". He will have a mutiny* on his hands soon if he's not careful.

Tuesday March 9th

FULL MOON

My schoolwork is plummeting down* to new depths. I only got five out of twenty for spelling. I think I might be anorexic*.

Wednesday March 10th

My father has asked me not to bring Pandora to the canal after school. He says he can't do anything with the lads after she has gone. It's true that she is stunningly* beautiful, but the lads will just have to learn self-control. I have had to learn it. She has refused to consummate our relationship*. Sometimes I wonder what she sees in me.

I live in daily terror of our relationship ending.

Thursday March 11th

Pandora and Pandora's mother have joined my mother's woman's group. No men or boys are allowed in our front room. My father had to be in charge of the crèche* in our dining room.

Rick Lemon's baby daughter Herod was crawling under the table shouting: "Tit! Tit!" My father kept telling Herod to shut up until I explained that Tit was Herod's mother's name. Herod is a very radical baby who never eats sweets and stays up until 2 a.m.

My father says that women ought to be at home cooking. He said it in a whisper so that he wouldn't be karate-chopped to death.

to spurn [spɜːn] **s.o.'s overture** ['əʊvəˌtjʊə] *fml.* not to want to talk to s.o. **to alienate** ['eɪljəneɪt] to make s.o. unfriendly **cruel** finding pleasure in causing other people pain **to bugger off** *BE sl. taboo* to go away **lefty** *BE inf. contempt.* believing in left-wing politics, being in favour of greater political changes **crap** *sl. contempt.* nonsense **mutiny** ['mjuːtɪnɪ] *G.* Meuterei **to plummet down** to fall down suddenly **anorexic** [ˌænə'reksɪk] (esp. of girls:) losing all appetite (*dys*lexic: unable to read and write correctly) **stunning** *here:* extraordinary **to consummate one's relationship** *fml.* to have sex with each other **crèche** [kreɪʃ] *BE from French* a place where children are looked after while their parents work

Friday March 12th

My father had a good day on the canal bank. He is almost through to the grass now. To celebrate he brought the skin-heads and punks round to our house for a glass of home-made beer. Mrs Singh and my mother looked shocked when the lads trooped* into our kitchen, but my father introduced Baz, Daz, Maz, Kev, Melv and Boz and my mother and Mrs Singh relaxed a bit.

Boz is going to help me fix the brakes on my bike, he is an expert bike-fixer. He has been stealing them since he was six.

Saturday March 13th

Boz offered me a sniff* of his glue* today, but I declined* it with thanks.

Sunday March 14th
THIRD IN LENT

All the women I know have gone to a rally* to protest about a woman's right to work. Mrs Singh has gone wearing a disguise*.

Saw Rick Lemon in the park, he was pushing Herod too high on a swing*. Herod was shouting: "Tit! Tit!"

Monday March 15th

I am loved by two women! Elizabeth Sally Broadway gave Victoria Louise Thomson a note in Science. It said: "Ask Adrian Mole if he wants to go out with me".

Victoria Louise Thomson (hereafter known as V.L.T.) passed on the message. I replied to V.L.T. in the negative.

Elizabeth Sally Broadway (hereafter known as E.S.B.) looked dead sad and started to cry into her bunsen burner.

It is really wonderful to know that Pandora and Elizabeth are both in love with me.

Perhaps I am not so ugly after all.

to troop to walk in a line **sniff** taking a drug through one's nose **glue** *G.* Klebstoff **to decline** to say "no" to, to refuse **rally** meeting **disguise** *G.* Verkleidung **swing** *here: G.* Schaukel

Tuesday March 16th

Pandora and E.S.B. have had a fight in the playground. I am disgusted with Pandora. At the last meeting of the Pink Brigade she swore to be a pacifist* all her life.

Pandora won! Ha! Ha! Ha!

Wednesday March 17th

ST PATRICK'S DAY. BANK HOLIDAY (IRELAND). MOON'S LAST QUARTER

Mr O'Leary was brought home by a police car at 10.30 p.m. Mrs O'Leary came over to ask my father if he would help her to get Mr O'Leary upstairs to bed. My father is still over there. I can hear the music and singing through the double-glazing*.

It is no joke when you need your sleep for school.

Thursday March 18th

I am reading *How Children Fail*, by John Holt. It is dead good. If I fail my O levels it will be all my parents' fault.

Friday March 19th

My creative English essay:

Spring, by A Mole

The trees explode into bud*, indeed some of them are in leaf. Their branches thrust* to the sky like drunken scarecrows*. Their trunks* writhe* and twist into the earth and form a plethora* of roots*. The brilliant sky hovers* uncertainly like a shy bride* at the door of her nuptial* chamber*. Birds wing* and scrape* their erratic* way into the cotton-wool clouds like drunken scarecrows. The translucent* brook* gurgles majestically towards its journey's end. "To the sea!" it cries, "to the sea!" it endlessly repeats.

pacifist s.o. who is strictly against violence and war **double-glazing** *G.* Doppelverglasung **bud** *G.* Knospe **to thrust** to push **scarecrow** ['skeəkrəʊ] *G.* Vogelscheuche **trunk** *G.* Baumstamm **to writhe** [raɪð] to twist the body as if being full of pain **plethora** ['pleθərə] *fml.* a greater number of things than one needs **root** the part of a plant that is under the ground **to hover** *G.* schweben **bride** a woman who has just married or is going to marry **nuptial** ['nʌpʃl] *here:* wedding **chamber** ['tʃeɪmbə] *arch.* bedroom **to wing** *literary* to fly **to scrape** to make an unpleasant noise **erratic** [ɪ'rætɪk] not regular, changing **translucent** [trænz'lu:snt] clear **brook** [brʊk] a small stream

A lonely boy, his loins* afire*, sits and watches his calm reflection in the torrential* brook. His heart is indeed heavy. His eyes fall on to the ground and rest on a wondrous* majestic many-hued* butterfly. The winged insect takes flight and the boy's eyes are carried far away until they are but a speck* on the red-hued sunset. He senses on the zephyr* a hope for mankind.

Pandora thinks this is the best thing I have ever written, but I know I have got a long way to go until I have learned my craft*.

Saturday March 20th
VERNAL EQUINOX

My mother has had all her hair cut off. She looks like one of Auntie Susan's inmates. She doesn't look a bit maternal* any more. I don't know whether to get her anything for Mother's Day or not. She was going on about it last night, saying it was a commercial* racket* fed by gullible* fools.

Sunday March 21st
FOURTH IN LENT. MOTHERING SUNDAY

11.30 a.m. Didn't get my mother anything so she has been in a bad mood all morning.

1 p.m. My father said, "If I were you, lad, I'd nip round* Cherry's and get your mother a card and present". He gave me two pounds so I got a card saying "Mummy I love you" (it was the only one left, just my luck), and five boxes of liquorice* allsorts* (going cheap because the boxes were squashed). She cheered up and didn't even mind when my father took a bunch of tulips round to grandma's and came back five hours later smelling of drink.

Pandora's mother was taken out and spoilt in a restaurant. I will do the same for my mother when I am famous.

loins the lower part of the body, around the sexual organs **afire** on fire **torrential** rushing violently **wondrous** ['wʌndrəs] *poetical* wonderful **hued** [hjuːd] *literary* coloured **speck** a very small piece, a spot **zephyr** ['zefə] *poetical* a soft west wind **craft** [krɑːft] *G.* Handwerk **maternal** [mə'tɜːnəl] like a mother **commercial** ['kə'mɜːʃl] *here contempt.* only produced to make money **racket** a business making money by taking advantage of people's naiveté **gullible** ['gʌləbl] being easily tricked, believing things too easily **to nip round** *inf.* to go quickly to s.o. or a place nearby **liquorice** ['lɪkərɪs] *G.* Lakritze **allsorts** a mixture

Monday March 22nd

I have catalogued* my bedroom library. I have got a hundred and fifty-one books, not counting the Enid Blytons*.

Tuesday March 23rd

I will be fifteen in eleven days. So I have only got to wait one year and eleven days to get married, should I want to.

Wednesday March 24th

The only thing that really worries me about my appearance* now is my ears. They stick out at an angle of ninety degrees. I have checked them with my geometry set so I know it is a scientific* fact.

Thursday March 25th
LADY DAY (QUARTER DAY). NEW MOON

I have had a spiritual* awakening*. Two nice men representing a religious group called the Sunshine People called at the house. They talked about how they alone could bring peace to the world. It is twenty pounds to join. I will get the money somehow. Nothing is too expensive where peace is concerned*.

Friday March 26th

Tried to persuade Pandora to join the Sunshine People. She was not swayed* by my arguments. They are calling round tomorrow to meet my parents and sign the agreement.

to catalogue ['kætəlɒg] to make a list of **Enid Blyton** a British writer of children's books (1897–1968) **appearance** *here:* what s.o. looks like **scientific** [ˌsaɪən'tɪfɪk] *G.* wissenschaftlich **spiritual** ['spɪrɪtjʊəl] *G.* geistig, seelisch **awakening** waking up **where s.th. is concerned** *here:* when one thinks of s.th. **to sway** to make people change their opinions

Saturday March 27th

The Sunshine People came at six o'clock. My father made them stand on the doorstep in the rain. Their robes got wet through. My father said they were trying to brainwash* a simple child. When they left my mother watched them walk up the cul-de-sac. She said, "They don't look very charismatic* now, they just look bloody wet". I wept a few tears. I think I was weeping out of relief—twenty quid is a lot of money.

Sunday March 28th

PASSION SUNDAY. BRITISH SUMMER TIME BEGINS

My father forgot to change the clocks last night so I was late for the Pink Brigade's meeting in Pandora's lounge. We voted to exclude Pandora's father from the meeting on the grounds of his extreme left-wing views. We have decided to back Roy Hattersley* in the expected fight for the leadership*.

Pandora has gone off Tony Benn* since she found out that he is a lapsed* aristocrat.

Claire Neilson introduced a new member, her name is Barbara Boyer. She is dead good-looking and also dead intelligent. She disagreed with Pandora over NATO's nuclear arms* policy*. Pandora had to concede* that China was an unknown factor. Pandora asked Claire Neilson not to bring Barbara again.

Monday March 29th

I ate my school dinner sitting next to Barbara Boyer. She is a truly wonderful girl. She pointed out that Pandora has got a lot of faults. I was forced to agree with her.

to brainwash *contempt.* to force people to believe s.th. by giving them no chance to think themselves **charismatic** [ˌkærɪzˈmætɪk] attracting a lot of people **Roy Hattersley** Deputy Leader of the British Labour Party since 1983 **leadership** *G.* Führung **Tony Benn** *cf. p. 160* **to lapse** to fall **nuclear arms** *G.* Atomwaffen **policy** [ˈpɒləsɪ] *G.* Politik **to concede** [kənˈsiːd] *here:* to admit, to say that s.th. is true

Tuesday March 30th

I am committing* non-sexual adultery* with Barbara. I am at the centre of an eternal* triangle*. Nigel is the only one to know: he has been sworn to secrecy.

Wednesday March 31st

Nigel has blabbed* it all over the school. Pandora spent the afternoon in matron's office.

Thursday April 1st
ALL FOOLS' DAY. MOON'S FIRST QUARTER

Barbara Boyer has ended our brief* *affaire*. I rang her up at the pet shop where she works part time cleaning the cages out. She said she couldn't bear to see the pain in Pandora's eyes. I asked her if it was an April Fools' joke, she said no and pointed out that it was after 12 a.m.

I have learnt an important lesson, because of lust I am without love.

I am fifteen tomorrow.

Had a shave to cheer myself up.

Friday April 2nd

I am fifteen, but legally I am still a child. There is nothing I can do today that I couldn't do yesterday. Worse luck!

Had seven cards from relations and three from friends. My presents were the usual load of Japanese rubbish*, though I did get a model aeroplane from Bert that was made in West Germany.

Pandora has ignored my birthday. I don't blame her. I betrayed* her trust*.

Boz, Baz, Daz, Maz, Kev and Melv came back from the canal and gave me the bumps*. Boz gave me a tube of glue* for my model aeroplane.

to commit adultery to have sex with s.o. who is married to another person **eternal** [iːˈtɜːnəl] having no end, lasting forever **triangle** [ˈtraɪæŋgl] *G.* Dreieck **to blab** *inf.* to tell a secret **brief** [briːf] short **rubbish** *here:* s.th. that is useless **to betray** *G.* verraten **trust** *here:* belief in s.o.'s good qualities **to give s.o. the bumps** holding s.o., esp. a child, by his/her arms and legs and swinging him/her into the air and back to the ground **glue** *G.* Klebstoff

Saturday April 3rd

8 a.m. Britain is at war with Argentina!!! Radio Four has just announced it. I am overcome with excitement. Half of me thinks it is tragic and the other half of me thinks it is dead exciting.

10 a.m. Woke my father up to tell him Argentina has invaded* the Falklands*. He shot out of bed because he thought the Falklands lay off the coast of Scotland. When I pointed out that they were eight thousand miles away he got back into bed and pulled the covers over his head.

4 p.m. I have just had the most humiliating* experience of my life. It started when I began to assemble* my model aeroplane. I had nearly finished it when I thought I would try an experimental sniff of glue. I put my nose to the undercarriage* and sniffed for five seconds, nothing spiritual happened but my nose stuck to the plane! My father took me to Casualty* to have it removed, how I endured* the laughing and sniggering* I don't know.

The Casualty doctor wrote "Glue Sniffer" on my outpatient's* card.

I rang Pandora; she is coming round after her viola* lesson. Love is the only thing that keeps me sane* …

to invade [ɪnˈveɪd] to enter a country with an army **the Falklands** *(cf. p. 164)* in 1982, Argentinian soldiers took over the Falkland Islands (the British won this war in June 1982, but only after many people had been killed on both sides) **humiliating** [hjuːˈmɪlɪeɪtɪŋ] *G.* demütigend **to assemble** to put together **undercarriage** [ˈʌndəˌkærɪdʒ] *G.* Fahrwerk, Fahrgestell **casualty** [ˈkæʒʊalti] *here: G.* (im Krankenhaus:) Notaufnahme **to endure** [ɪnˈdjʊə] to bear s.th. calmly **to snigger** to laugh at s.o. else's bad luck **outpatient** a patient who does not have to stay in hospital over night, but can still live at home **viola** [vɪˈəʊlə] an instrument like a violin, though a little larger **sane** [seɪn] not mad, healthy